Scarlett MccGwire is a freelance journalist, and she also runs a successful communications consultancy. She is the author of *Kim's Story – A Fight for Life* and *Best Companies for Women*, as well as educational books for secondary-school pupils, and she edited *Transforming Moments*, an anthology for teenagers, published by Virago. She lives in North London with her partner Christian and their assortment of three children.

Women Who Love Men Who Kill

Scarlett MccGwire

First published in Great Britain in 1994 by
True Crime
an imprint of Virgin Publishing Ltd
332 Ladbroke Grove
London W10 5AH

ISBN 0 86369 736 4

A catalogue record for this title is available from the
British Library

Typeset by TW Typesetting, Plymouth, Devon
Printed and bound in Great Britain by
Cox & Wyman Ltd, Reading, Berks

for my parents

Contents

Acknowledgements

This book has been completely dependent on the help and co-operation of others. The most important people are the women who allowed me to interview them, spilled out their feelings, fears and anxieties and let them go into print. Many of these women were contacted by Shirl Mahy from Aftermath, who persuaded them that I was trustworthy; thank you. There are also the many who gave me ideas, help and suggestions: Wendy Morris from the Trauma After Care Trust; Anna Reynolds, Duncan Campbell, Henry Hodge, Madeleine Colvin, Nick Davies, Barbara Gunnell, my agent, Jane Gregory and Cheryl Crowther. Kerry Heard transcribed half the tapes. Christian, as always, provided emotional and subbing support, and the children, Molly, Pascoe and Misha, expect to be mentioned.

Introduction

What is the fatal attraction that murderers hold for some women? How does the mother of a killer cope with the knowledge that her son has taken another's life? And could you stand by your man knowing that he has killed?

Women Who Love Men Who Kill sets out to answer those questions by asking the women themselves. This is not a book about the celebrity-case murderers' wives such as Sonia Sutcliffe and Kate Kray. Their stories are well, and often, told elsewhere. Neither is it about those so-called 'murder groupies' who regularly write love letters to convicted killers such as Peter Sutcliffe, the 'Yorkshire Ripper'. It is about those hundreds of women who criss-cross the country every week to visit their husbands, lovers, brothers, fathers or sons in prison. These women are very ordinary, but they lead extraordinary lives because of the actions of their loved ones. They could be anyone you know, and in these frank and intimate interviews, they tell in their own words how they survived the unthinkable.

A wife of a killer has usually played no part in her husband's crime, yet has the double burden of seeing her man through the jail sentence and of dealing with the guilt of what he has done. Often she is seen by her community as sharing the blame for the victim's death. The strain is usually intolerable. Only two of the women I interviewed for this book managed to stand by their man, and it is no coincidence that they both come from communities which have a tradition of staying loyal to those in prison. Kathy, born into a North London criminal family, was well used to her father going down; when her husband, 'a vicious, knife-happy little sod', was sent to prison for manslaughter, she knew what was expected of her. She supported her man while the other members of the fraternity helped her financially. Similarly, Sinéad comes from a Republican area of West Belfast where support for Republican prisoners is a way of life, and where those convicted of killing are regarded not as murderers but as political prisoners; many of her own relatives had been in prison before her husband was convicted of shooting two soldiers. Supporting what he did, seeing it as part of the armed struggle, Sinéad was given a tremendous amount of support by her family and when she chose to leave her man – albeit temporarily – she had to deal with widespread disapproval.

There is a lot of suspicion surrounding those women who choose to become involved with men already in prison for murder. There is the feeling that they are attracted to the dubious 'glamour' of a murder sentence, or that they want a relationship that avoids all confrontation with reality: after all, you can promise undying love to a man behind bars but you need never put up with the humdrum everyday details of a life together. It is certainly true that there are those who are strongly attracted to the perpetrators of violent crime: Peter Sutcliffe gets many marriage proposals and Harry Roberts, who has been in jail since 1968 for the killing of a policeman and should have long faded from public attention, gets letters from women explaining in detail the erotic acrobatics they would perform for him. There are various theories to explain the phenomenon, none of them flattering to the women themselves. The authorities are also concerned that these men are making use of slightly naïve women: a prisoner is far more likely to be released early if he has a loving wife who will, it is hoped, keep him on the straight and narrow once outside; and while he is in jail, having someone to bring him money and cigarettes and organise things is always useful. As a result, women who marry prisoners are vetted thoroughly, their lifestyles and values questioned, and they often feel like criminals although, of course, they themselves have done nothing wrong.

Yet these women all stress that they have individual reasons for their relationships. Each one is careful to emphasise that they did not fall in love with a killer, but with a man: a man who had made one mistake – a terrible mistake, an unforgivable mistake, but still a mistake. They came to terms with their man's crime by downgrading it. In each case, they say, the man had changed or matured and the woman felt that he was not the same person who had taken another's life. Of these women, only Queenie, whose marriage failed, felt that her own life would ever have been at risk from her husband.

Unlike wives and lovers, however, mothers, daughters and sisters have less chance to walk away. Both mothers interviewed here believe in their sons' innocence, even after they had confessed to the killings, arguing that they had been fitted up by the police. Indeed, one of the strategies for staying loyal is placing the blame elsewhere: a son might have been brought up in a family with an alcohol problem; another might have been led astray by others. These women are tortured by the 'what ifs' – what if one had persuaded her son to get married and settle down rather than move to London and become involved in politics; what if another had not turned her brother away when he needed to talk about his marriage . . .? They are torn by an almost unthinkable clash of loyalties and emotions: no one wants to love a bad man and certainly no one wants to have brought one up.

For all these women, the initial shock of hearing that their man has killed is only the first thing they will have to overcome. The strain of the trial and its attendant publicity is enormous, and is followed by years of visiting in bleak communal rooms where privacy is minimal. Visiting rooms may be clean and prison officers friendly, but the system offers no opportunity for privacy: people desperately try to squeeze the minutiae of relationships into two hours. Conversations are governed by the clock, and throughout the time allotted visitors feel they are treated with suspicion, as if they themselves were criminals. It is surely in the interest of the state for the relationships of convicted men to survive – it has often been shown that those with no outside support make the most difficult prisoners and are highly likely to reoffend – but the prison system is not designed to make this easy. The pressure of visiting – prisoners can be moved across the country at short notice, often hundreds of miles from their home town – is not the only financial burden for the women. The cost of supporting and visiting a man in jail can run into hundreds of pounds a year, a double burden if the man was also the family breadwinner and his contribution to the family has disappeared. Faced with these pressures, it is unsurprising that wives and girlfriends need to make a life of their own from which their man is increasingly removed. The Home Office does not keep any statistics on the number of prisoners who get divorced, saying that it is a personal matter, but it is thought to be high.

Once the man is released – and as lifers are held at the Home Secretary's pleasure, release dates are never defined – things do not get any easier. Fewer and fewer employers are willing to give any work to a convicted murderer, and more often than not the woman is also unable to find a job. Through no fault of their own, these women – and their children – are condemned to a life of grinding poverty. There is also no real end to a life sentence: prisoners are released only on licence and for the rest of their lives are answerable to the Home Office; one misdemeanour and they are back inside.

There is a lifeline for many of these women, which came about when Shirl Mahy accompanied the mother of a murdered boy through the grisly trial. One day her friend approached an equally tragic figure in court – the mother of the murderer – to offer comfort from one bereaved parent to another. Her words were the catalyst for Aftermath, but they could also sum up this book: 'There are so many victims.'

Every woman in this book tells her own story in her own words. Many names and locations have been changed to protect the privacy of some. The details and emotions described are very real. The women who love men who kill speak for themselves.

Part 1

Women Whose Men Became Killers

When I was writing this book many people asked me if I would stand by my man if he killed anybody. When I answered that it depended on the circumstances of the crime I was deemed to be disloyal. Yet if I discovered that he had planned and executed a series of murders he would not be the man I thought I was in love with. However, I know that he could lose control if our children were threatened; that he has shouted at drivers and thumped cars who have used our small street as a racetrack when he and the children were trying to cross the road.

But these women are not the Sonia Sutcliffes of this world – they did not wake up one morning to discover the man they loved was a mass murderer. The men's crimes were in character. Kathy's husband always was 'a knife-happy little sod', so a bit of 'eyeballing' and 'verbal' between two groups of young men in a Wimpy Bar turning into a killing outside was tragic but unsurprising. Sinéad knew her husband was politically active and supported the Republican movement in Northern Ireland and wondered if he was 'militarily active' – the euphemism for being a member of the IRA. When he was arrested for killing two soldiers she was not surprised. One could say that Chrissie caused her lover to become a murderer, for she paid him to kill her husband. He had told her he was a member of an international hit squad, which was a fantasy, but she had believed him to be a killer.

1

Andrea appears to be the odd one out, for she married her husband after he had served his term in Northern Ireland for the Welsh Guards. However, when she married him, she had no idea he had even been a soldier let alone killed somebody. Her man's killing was a question of doing his job. It was not a criminal act. Andrea's story shows that she is living with a deeply disturbed man and, according to Wendy Morris at the Trauma After Care Trust, his disturbance was caused by his experiences in Northern Ireland.

TACT treats soldiers and their families from the Gulf War, the Falklands War and Northern Ireland. The cases they treat show that even killing which has been sanctioned, indeed actively encouraged, by society can have a devastating effect on the perpetrators and their families.

The women in this section discovered what happened when their men went to the extremes of their characters.

Kathy Bailey

Kathy Bailey comes from the criminal fraternity. Her father, Reg Dudley, was a thief, extremely well respected by all his North London colleagues for his ability to get through the toughest anti-burglar devices. When he decided he could no longer take the physical exertion required he became a successful 'fence'. In 1975 he was found guilty of murdering another criminal, Billy Moseley, and given life. The case, known as the torso murder because that was the only part of the victim's body which was found, was, at the time, the longest trial in British criminal history. There are those who have studied the case and believe that Reg Dudley and his co-accused, Bobby Maynard, are innocent and were 'fitted up'. There have been many campaigns to free Reg Dudley.

I was introduced to Kathy by one of the journalists who has argued her father's innocence in 1983, at the time her husband was doing time for conspiracy to commit armed robbery. When I asked her if she could help me find any women to interview for this book she pointed out that her first husband had been found guilty of manslaughter. Her council flat is full of ill-assorted animals, rescued strays; the door is kept open and she is at everybody's beck and call. She is gentle and vulnerable.

Being a daughter of the criminal aristocracy she loved the glamour and money that went with it. However, visiting a man in jail is hard and lonely and the glamour began to look rather empty and shallow.

She now lives with a musician on a council estate in Islington, regularly visiting her father and waiting for him to come out.

It was Easter 1968 and I was only nineteen. I was living in Finsbury Park in North London and working in a betting shop, taking in money and paying out money and learning to settle bets. I left school, which I hated, at fifteen. I hung around, sometimes taking little jobs. There were millions of jobs. I could start one job one day, not like it, and go find another one to start the next day. I had no real interest in anything other than having a good time.

In those days, it was still safe to congregate on the streets without the fear that you have nowadays. We all used to hang around Highbury Corner and lark about over the fields. Johnny Dan was the local comedian, a jokey person and a prankster. His nickname was Donut. He was looked up to because he mixed with an older crowd. When the older boys came by they were treated like little heroes. He had a nice sense of humour, a nice smile and I was flattered when he chatted me up. He was 21 and was an asphalter, working with somebody laying roads or roofing.

I started sleeping with him and I was terrified of getting pregnant, so I thought I had better hurry up and get married. The Pill was not readily available to young people in those days. I married him in the early summer, about two months after we met, without really knowing the first thing about him.

It was a register office wedding, but a big one because my dad had money and he laid on a lavish spread. It was a good party. However, even that morning, as we pulled up at the register office, John got out of the car and spewed everywhere from the after-effects of his stag night. I remember looking at him and thinking, 'Oh my God, that's no way to be on your wedding morning.'

I should have run off there and then. My best friend said to me: 'Look, if you want to go, we'll go now. We'll keep driving to Scotland. You don't have to go through with this.'

I said: 'I can't. There's all these people here. All that food.' I went through it like a robot, because I did not want to do it.

For our honeymoon we went to my father's caravan in

Clacton-on-sea. John had already booked a holiday with some friends of his before we had arranged to get married so he went off to Spain with his mates while I drove down with a couple of my friends to meet them there. It was not any sort of a romantic honeymoon, it was ten people having a whopping time. It was good fun.

We were lucky and got a flat around the corner from my family home. I was only married a week when I thought, I've made a terrible mistake. I had not even got to really know him. It was only after we were married that I started finding out things about him. I only married him for a licence to sleep with him. He was nice and had a wonderful personality, but there was another side to him; a knife-happy, vicious little sod. At one stage he thought about trying it on me, when he realised that the marriage was not going to work, but I never felt in any serious danger.

I had not known John for long. Most of the kids I grew up with and hung around with I knew from schooldays, but John just came by one night and flirted with me and it went on from there. He did not have any close family. He was adopted and had lost contact with his adoptive parents. Obviously there was a very sad story behind the comedian, a story I did not even know about, a sad little boy. There is probably a story to why he was a bit knife-happy. He obviously hid it all by acting the clown to everybody. He was known to be knife-happy: he had threatened people with a knife before, but because I did not really know him, I had never seen it.

Being still very young, I decided to get out of it as quickly as possible. By the end of the summer I had gone back home to my family so many times that, in the end, my dad told me to go back and throw him out because it was a waste of the flat. So that is what I did.

When I told my dad I didn't want to be in the marriage any more he said: 'Why did you get married in the first place? You know I would have let you live with him.'

I remember thinking, no, you bloody well would not have done. My dad had agreed to it because he had also got married at nineteen and assumed I was old enough and responsible.

My dad ran the family because my mum was an alcoholic and the drink eventually killed her. Her alcoholism may have started because he was in and out of prison so much. There were years when I thought my dad was to blame for everything, and other times when I thought my mum might have been to blame. The older I get I think it was probably six of one and half a dozen of the other. I think they really loved each other.

My mum came to the wedding but she was so drunk that she didn't remember anything about it. There was no communication with her. She was permanently pissed. I would have silly little conversations but nothing in-depth – for the last twenty years of her life she was never sober long enough. I have only ever been able to have heart-to-hearts with my dad and my sister.

Within a couple of days of John leaving I heard there was some trouble about a stabbing in Holborn. He had gone out with a couple of friends for the evening to a Wimpy Bar, which no longer exists, at the top end of Shaftesbury Avenue towards the Seven Dials. There was some sort of a staring match in the Wimpy Bar between his group and another bunch of men, which had gone on to a bit of verbal. A fight ensued and my husband stabbed one of them. He came back home but I had no idea of the seriousness of it until two or three weeks later, when the police came to my flat about my father, who was a jewellery fence. John was there when they searched the flat and they told him there was a warrant out for his arrest. He was taken to Brixton and within a couple of days the guy he stabbed died.

At the beginning I did not take any of it in because I did not realise how serious it was, even when he was charged: it was somebody I did not know and something I was not part of. I just shut out of my mind what he had done and felt sorry for him because he was in this trouble.

At the Old Bailey the man's wife stood up and screamed

out that she would get him one day for killing her husband. I think then the full impact hit me. Somebody had actually been killed and he had a family and he was young and so many other lives had been destroyed in the process. None of that had even occurred to me during the arrest and while we waited for the trial.

At the same time as John got three years for the killing, my father got five years for receiving stolen jewellery. I remember visiting John in the cells at the Old Bailey after he was sentenced. He was thinking of appealing and I was disgusted with him. I thought, you ought to count your lucky stars that you have only got three years and go on and do the time. Having heard this woman and then listening to him bellyaching that he had got three years, I was disgusted with the whole business. But I lived in an environment where you just carried on and you did not leave people in trouble like that. To me, prison was just part of life; if you got caught that was where you went.

From then on I was scheming all the time to get out of the marriage, even though I was visiting him like good wives had to do in those days. I was forever working out how to get out of it. He was on remand for six months before his case came up and did another eighteen months after that. When he came out, I picked him up from the prison, got him home and said: 'There's your clothes, there are your belongings. I'm off. 'Bye.'

People did not do that in those days and I was considered a very bad person. What John had done was not considered a wrongdoing, except by the family of the guy he had killed.

However, afterwards, a lot of people like my grandmother and auntie told me they had thought I was stark raving mad getting married in the first place, but had not liked to say anything. I don't remember anybody saying afterwards: 'Oh what a shame, he was such a nice bloke.' I think everyone in my family breathed a sigh of relief.

John really suffered in prison. He is not a man who can do time. When I went to visit him, he tried to be chirpy, but I knew that he just couldn't do it. It was killing him, short as it was. I bumped into him once about ten years later and he was very sarcastic and nasty to me, and obviously still hated me. I heard that he went off with a rich Dutch woman so I don't think he was bitter about losing me, but he was bitter about me not standing by him.

I had been brought up in the criminal world and being part of it is like showbusiness. It is divided into different divisions and after John, I had relationships with armed robbers, so I was mingling and mixing with the first division. There are also all these little Godfather types, the really old criminals who are still about. When they come into a room, everyone shows them respect.

There is an awful lot of money. They get the money and you have all these nice things and go on great holidays. At the drop of a hat, you can go anywhere you like. But all that pales when you think of how long they do in prison. In the old days, if a woman was struggling someone would always help her out, as the years go by, all that is changing because so many people are in prison and so many people out here are skint.

My dad would have been up there in the first division. He was not an armed robber but he was a brilliant thief; he could get in and out of secure buildings. He had the most respect because the few people who knew of his exploits knew what he was good at.

The other hierarchy apart from the armed robbers was the clever ones who used brain rather than muscle. Dad reached an age when he couldn't scale up walls, so he was into buying and selling. Women were judged by how many fur coats they had and how many diamonds on their fingers. We were not supposed to have any sort of intellect, just to look beautiful and drip nice things.

In 1974 a guy called Billy Moseley came home from prison. He had been in for a small thing, to do with stolen cheque-books I think. There were not so many credit cards in those days – they were only starting to find their way through – and Bill used to work with cheques. He had done about eighteen months inside. I knew him as part of the older generation, although he drank in one of the pubs that my little crowd used to go to. He was more of an acquaintance than a friend.

A day or two after Bill came home from prison he disappeared, literally disappeared off the face of the earth. Rumours started to go around that his disappearance was serious. People said he had had some sort of an affair with a married woman before he had gone inside. The woman's husband, who had been in prison himself, had found out about it and, as he had been released before Bill, had made arrangements to see Bill and discuss it. Apparently the woman had told the husband that the relationship was over, but he had traced a letter from a pad which showed that she had been writing to Bill regularly while he was in prison. He obviously thought she was going to carry on the relationship.

The man's story was that he had made this meeting with Bill, but Bill had never turned up and that was the end of it. The only interest in Bill in the early days was within criminal circles, because the police had not been informed that he was missing. Then Bill's best friend, Bobby Maynard, who had gone into partnership with my father over the previous couple of years in buying and selling stolen jewellery and silver, became even more concerned about Bill. He made his own enquiries and found that the story was not just a rumour. So Bobby got Bill's ex-wife, Anne, to report Bill missing.

About a year later, a guy called Mickey Cornwall came home from prison and also disappeared. Eight weeks later, his body was found buried in a grave in Hertfordshire. He had been shot in the head.

Mickey was from the bank robbery era and he had been serving quite a long sentence, but when he had come home all those people he had associated with had been put away or were in hiding. It was the time of Bertie Small, the supergrass who had reported all his friends to the police.

Mickey was lost: he had finally got out of prison but none of his friends were around, so he was trying to find people who would mix with him and do the same type of work.

I felt sorry for Mick, because I had a boyfriend who was a bank robber and was in prison, and I could imagine what it was going to be like when he finally came out. Mickey was obviously having difficulties, having been in prison for such a long time, and could not find his feet anywhere. I used to have a chat and a drink with him and I thought he was ever so nice. I ended up in bed with him one night, but as far as I was concerned there was no harm done and it was no big love affair. He met somebody I thought was really nice and I used to drink with them as a couple. They seemed well suited.

When Mickey disappeared and was subsequently found dead, the police came and interviewed me at my house. They said that they had been told that I was his girlfriend and they had come to break the bad news. I explained that he had been with another girl for well over six months. She had mentioned that she hadn't seen him for a couple of weeks and that she was worried, but I'd told her not to worry because I assumed he had got some money and gone off.

The police asked me to go with them and break the news to her. When we got to the girl's house, her mother came home from work and the police said they wanted to take her to a Hertfordshire police station to interview her, because that force was dealing with the murder. Her mother wanted to go with her, because she was obviously distressed, but they would not allow it. They wanted me to go instead. It was not until we got to Hertfordshire that I realised I was the main one they wanted for questioning, because I was interviewed by the head of Hertfordshire Police, while the other girl was interviewed separately by a less senior officer.

I heard that this murder was being linked to Billy Moseley's disappearance over a year earlier and that the police were pulling in people from all over North London for questioning about both murders. People were being asked how well they knew my dad and me. For several months after that, we got lots of messages and phone calls to say that the police were looking to build up a case against my dad for both murders. In those days, even in the criminal world, if you had not committed a murder you really didn't let that sort of thing bother you. You always thought that with a murder they would get the right people. So my dad didn't pay much attention to the warnings.

In January 1976 the police staged a massive raid in North London at five in the morning and arrested twenty people. Seven of them were charged with various things from murder to conspiracy to cause bodily harm. My father, Reg Dudley, and Bobby Maynard, his partner, were charged with the two murders. Bobby Maynard's brother and one of my dad's old pals from years back were charged with lesser offences and a local guy who had been chauffeuring my dad, as my dad had lost his licence, and who was involved in odd jobs and petty crime, was also charged with one of the murders. The man whose wife had been having the affair with Bill, and who was nothing to do with our circle at all, was also charged with Bill's murder. I was charged with conspiracy to commit grievous bodily harm.

So seven of us appeared at various times at the committal in the Magistrates' Court and waited for trial at the Old Bailey. Most of the evidence against all of us amounted to the interviews with the police when a solicitor had not been allowed to be there, where we had made what they considered to be semi-confessions. Some other evidence came out of Brixton Prison when the men were on remand and had apparently admitted to other prisoners that they had done it. There were also coincidences, like one man saying he had seen my dad have a fight with Billy Moseley ten years before in a pub and had heard my dad say, 'I'll get you for this.' It turned out that this man had a string of convictions for buggery and child abuse and was waiting to go back up for sentencing. It was obvious that the police had said: 'Say what we tell you to say and you will get off.'

Another bit of evidence was that a girl of fifteen, who had lived in a house where Mickey Cornwall had once lodged, had said that Mickey had gone off one day and that shortly afterwards two men came looking for him. She later picked out, from photographs rather than an identification parade, my dad and Bob. That was all very dodgy, and even if they had been looking for him, Mickey was seen out and about for another two months after that. Anyway, my dad knew where Mickey lived and had even dropped him off there after going for a drink.

That was the entire evidence for the prosecution. I know it would never stand up now, but in those days Sir Robert Mark had given high-ranking police officers *carte blanche* to clean up London. That was exactly what they were doing. By fair means or foul, they put people away.

In its day it was the longest murder trial in history. There were seven defendants, twelve different charges, and so many other people either directly or indirectly involved that it just went on and on.

When I remember those times, it seemed an eternity. The trial lasted seven months and I still cannot believe that we lived through it. I don't think I could live through it again. I was in custody for four months and then I got bail at the committal hearing, when they realised there was virtually no evidence against me and that nobody was living in fear of me. I had been put up very much as 'the father's daughter' who was dangerous and would do anything to keep her father out of prison. Those were the police objections to bail. It was not until the actual committal for trial that the magistrate heard the evidence. He asked one or two witnesses if they were scared of me, to which one woman laughed and replied, 'No. Kathy wouldn't hurt a fly.' Then I got bail.

Until then I was in Holloway, which was awful. It was the old castle – the lovely modern building had not yet been erected. At one time I was on the sick women's wing, which was called C1. It was notorious for child-killers, very sick women and those on fairly serious charges. They

12

mixed convicted and remand prisoners together. In fact C1 was all right for me because I had a single cell. At one time I was put in the normal remand wing and shared a cell with two others.

I am told that the new Holloway is different. In those days all you ever heard was screaming; women would sell their soul for a dog-end. You only had to put your soap or your toothpaste down and it would disappear. It was nothing like the lovely camaraderie in men's prisons. The sickening thing was that you would get someone in there who had been stealing brassières out of Woolworth's and she would be crying her eyes out because she was being sent home.

The extremes in there were just pathetic: I remember a fourteen-year-old being put down on C1 because they just did not know what to do with her. She was underage but she was not going to be accepted in a young persons' place because Holloway was more secure. There were lots of odd characters; some very nice, some not so nice. It was just total chaos in there, really.

I was found guilty of conspiracy to cause grievous bodily harm and got a two-year suspended sentence. My dad got life with a recommended fifteen years minimum, and Bobby Maynard got the same. I was devastated.

Afterwards we campaigned. We did everything to show it was a miscarriage of justice. The campaign to free George Davis, a guy who had been fitted up for a local job, showed us the way. They mounted a campaign which got massive publicity, including stopping a test match by digging up the wicket, and got enough momentum going to get him out, but once he was rearrested in the course of an armed robbery, nobody cared any more who was innocent.

The first year was spent getting ready for the appeal. There is always another step. No matter how devastated you are you have to pick yourself up and get on to the next stage. I think in my heart I wasn't so sure that it would be easy to get them out, having seen what had happened at the Old Bailey. I don't know that I believed that much any

13

more in justice. All the families at the time were saying that we had got the appeal coming up; the judges will throw this out, there should never have been a conviction. The appeal came up in 1979 and it was turned down. So between 1979 and the mid-eighties we did everything we could to campaign. A journalist wrote a book about it. One small television programme was made before the appeal went out, but other than a little bit of comment on the day people always lost interest. Recently a documentary was made lasting nearly an hour which caused a lot of comment for a week, but even that has gone by the board now.

We had hopes with the ESDA test. This involves going over police interview notes using a type of tracing which shows whether they have written things down verbatim or added little bits by themselves. Because we knew that our notes were false, we asked for them so that they could be tested, but we were told they had been destroyed. Any time something comes up, we seem to be stymied by the powers that be.

I always knew my father didn't do it. Our close friends knew too. But there were people on the periphery who loved to believe it and they were probably the rumour-mongers who started it in the first place. Bobby Maynard got a lot of sympathy because people liked him, but my dad was a hard man anyway. Some people said to me: 'Look what he did in his younger days. He is capable of it.' He did have a record of violence; of course he is capable. They would not have fitted up a vicar, they had to find someone likely.

I always felt I had to apologise for it, even though neither my dad nor I had done anything. About two years ago, after he had been inside for fifteen years, I got sick of it. It is just the looks people give you. They don't even have to say anything to you. You see people looking and you know exactly what they are thinking: that you did it. I would go to one place and people would put their arms round me and tell me, 'It's all right, kid, we know you are all right. Please God your dad and Bob get out soon,' and all that. But they never do anything to help you, because they don't want to put somebody else in it. The most support I got was from the people who actually knew who did it. Those who aren't so sure, they are the ones who give you the eye, the downcast eye.

It wrecked my life. Even if you are trying to live a normal life you cannot get a job with a conviction for conspiracy to cause grievous bodily harm and it was a very famous case in its day. I could only get menial jobs, so that's what I did.

Every waking hour, there was no time when it was out of my mind. For the first five or six years, trying every channel for campaign work, organising protests and writing to influential people just took up a lot of time. Then I had to start coming to terms with the fact that nothing was going to happen, and if anything did happen it was certainly not going to happen overnight. I was proved right as we are now seventeen years on. I tried to keep an even balance in my life, but it is the same as having somebody in hospital: even if you try to get into a routine, your life literally revolves around that person, visiting them and trying to keep up their morale over all those years.

I have watched all these cases come and go: the Guildford Four, the Birmingham Six, Tottenham. It was great for them, but I am beginning to resent these cases, wondering whether it is political or whether there is some sort of rule somewhere that says it does not matter about right and wrong, you are not coming out for so many years. The longer it goes on the more I think that the reason why they have not been let out of prison is entirely political.

All that has had much more effect than my husband killing somebody. That was something I pushed out of my head the day I walked out of the door. On those rare occasions when I reflect on my past and my husband killing that guy, I really only ever think about that woman screaming in the courtroom. But I certainly didn't think

15

about her for the first ten years after it happened. It is only now, when I reflect on lives that have been ruined – because mine was ruined too – that I realise what that poor woman went through. It shattered her life.

If I could get my dad out I would be at peace with the world.

Christine Buckley

Christine Buckley was found guilty of conspiring to murder her husband in 1986 and given a life sentence. She had paid her lover to kill him. She had been a middle-class, reasonably well-off woman who owned a snack bar and a dress shop, and who had friends in the police force, when she was suddenly thrown into the demeaning, shocking world of the prison system. She was sent to Durham Prison, which is for Category A prisoners – the highest risk group, including murderers and terrorists. She thought the conditions and treatment of the women inhumane. However, she says she met some remarkable women in there, many of whom became her friends. Among them was Judith Ward who was released after seventeen years when the Appeal Court found that she was wrongfully convicted of blowing up a coach on the M62 in 1975. Another of those friends, who now runs Inside Time, *a newspaper for prisoners, suggested that I contact Christine. She had served seven years of her sentence and had been transferred to Styall Prison. I found her to be friendly, utterly candid and charming. She was smartly dressed with her hair well styled; she made it clear that she was taking prison on her terms and was not going to allow it to erode her self-respect. She told me she was not going to play 'the system's mind games' even though she knew this was an attitude which was going to stall her chances of parole. Her greatest regret is that she has lost contact with her daughters who no longer visit; but she still sees many of her old friends. She is 47 and hopes to be released in 2001. She claims she is still in love with her husband, despite having him killed.*

I suppose it all began one November night in 1980. I was living in Wrexham and I believed I was happily married. I had two wonderful daughters but I was slightly bored. I had a girlfriend whose husband was in Saudi Arabia and she was seeing this guy while he was away. She asked me if I wanted to come out with them both.

I remember it was a filthy night and I had not eaten before we went out. We met at eight o'clock and had a few drinks, which went straight to my head. Then I saw Albert.

He was just the most wonderful guy I had ever seen. I was hit by him. I stayed the night and loved him from then on. Within four weeks I was living with him and just over twelve months later, on 22 December 1981, we were married. He had been divorced seven years earlier, and had a son and daughter from that marriage, and was living with someone who left him when I became involved with him.

I left my home and my children for him. The girls were eleven and thirteen. It was a horrendous decision but for their stability it was the right thing to do. I was completely demented.

When I met Albert he had retired, although he was only 45. I was working for the Welsh Water Authority in Mold, but when we decided to move to Northwich I found it too far to travel. Albert and I decided to start a business in Northwich called The Lunchbox, which provided sandwiches and snacks as midday meals for people. Albert really loved transport, so he set up a company carrying stuff. After two years I opened a dress shop in Northwich, Cheshire and we lived in the flat above it. We also kept The Lunchbox on.

There were problems from the start, but I was absolutely besotted with him. I never wanted to return to my first husband Alan, who was a truly nice man, because I only wanted Albert.

I would occasionally see my girls, but it was always difficult because Albert would get so jealous. He made it clear he was not happy whenever they visited. He just could not stand me seeing them. If we were sitting having a meal or watching the television he just ignored them. He would go searching in their rooms, prying among their possessions. He was so horrid to them. He never hit them; it was not physical, it was mental. He hated them, absolutely hated them. He was jealous, but at the time I could not see that. All I could see was this man going on about my daughters.

There was always one problem or another with Albert. If it was not my daughters, he would complain about my staff. There never seemed to be any peace. Once I tried to divorce him. I went to a solicitor, but then I backed out. I just could not face it.

He had been reared as a Salvationist. After National Service he did not go back. During our early marriage Albert went out drinking and socialising like I did, like a normal person. However, around early 1983, after his father died he went back to being a Salvationist. He joined The Salvation Army and in fact joined the band, playing the trombone for them. I was forbidden to drink, wear jeans or smoke. I tried to go along with it. It was brilliant at the beginning, when I was quite docile and I would do anything for him. But bloody hell, enough is enough. When I started saying 'no' he could not stand it.

I started getting pissed off at being used as a doormat. It went on for at least two years. He was retired, and I was working full time, as well as looking after his mother, while he did nothing. He would go and have coffee with his friends, staying out till all hours, while I would be the poor little wife at home.

One night he said he was staying in our cottage in Wales, but he changed his mind and came back to find me lying in bed with a cigarette and a glass of sherry. He was livid.

He just used to shout at me, telling me how inefficient I was and how stupid I was. I wanted to be loved and he said I could not be loved because love had to be earned and I did not earn it.

I used to have screaming turns and I would hit him. I was frightened of his reaction, I was so scared of him, yet I still loved him. We both used to assault each other. I would kick him, scratch his face and throw things at him. He used to hit me quite often, leaving bruises. Once he tried to strangle me with a scarf. Around Christmas 1985 Albert and I had an argument in The Lunchbox one evening. I ended up on the floor and Albert gave me a good kicking.

When my daughters came to live with me for a while he even talked me into agreeing to charge them rent. Trying to love all of them just tore me apart. He wanted me to either live with my daughters or live with him. He called my girls rubbish and ill-mannered.

After one particularly bad time when the children were staying and Albert had been awful to them, I went out with one of the girls who used to work for me. We were sitting having a drink with some of the guys we knew, when one of them, Trevor, said something about paraquat.

I said: 'Hey Trev, have you got any over? You can give Albert a dose.'

One of the guys, Dave, asked if I was serious.

I replied: 'Yes, I'm serious.'

I had fancied Dave for quite a while. His wife was the headmistress of the local school and he was into buying and selling second-hand cars. He worked at the garage round the corner and used to come into the shop and sit and have coffee. Albert and I were arguing a lot and I would think how easy it was just flirting with Dave.

He certainly was not the first man I had slept with since marrying Albert. I was just a whore. In my working life I was always having affairs with guys. The problem was that sex with Albert had stopped. He was ten years my senior, from a generation where sex was not talked about. So we never talked about why he was not interested in sex.

Going to bed with Dave seemed very natural as we planned how he would kill Albert. The affair was terribly exciting, as I was always waiting for the phone calls and for him to come round, or when his wife was out on a Wednesday night Dave would ask me to pop round and I would.

After we had been to bed a few times I started to go off

him. It was not like falling in love with Albert; nobody could ever come up to his standard.

Dave told me that he was a professional hit man for an organisation that had people all over the world. I had to pay him £3,500 to kill Albert. I paid him the money – I had to take a bank loan to get it. We pretended it was a business deal, and to make it look right he let me have a Peugeot van. He also said that his organisation would buy Albert's transport business as companies like that were very useful for getting rid of large sums of money. But his stories about the organisation were all make-believe. Now I cannot believe that I took him seriously. He was just a car salesman with a gift for the gab. That is obvious when I look back, but I did not see it at the time.

Dave told me that because he was seeing me he had got his knuckles rapped. Normally he would have got someone else to bump Albert off, but he was going to have to do it himself.

My psychiatrist says he is a pillock and it was unfortunate that we were in the wrong place at the wrong time.

Albert and I had a cottage in Wales, where we often used to go for weekends. Dave insisted that I took him to the cottage and he looked in every nook and cranny and found a gun in my wardrobe. I had hidden it there because my stepson used to play with it and I did not want him to find it. Dave took it away with him, saying Albert might use it against him. Looking back at it I cannot believe I was so naive and gullible. Then we went up to bed.

I know it sounds very odd, but even though I was planning to kill him I still desperately loved Albert. During the time I was planning to kill him he left me and I went round and begged him to come back. Yet all this time I was seeing Dave. I think I was mad. I cannot imagine how I survived: trying to run a business, having an affair, trying to get Albert back and trying to negotiate the bank loan for Dave so he could kill him.

After four weeks Albert and I started going out to dinner together. He sold the cottage in Wales, where he had been living when he left me, and moved next door to Trevor, which was about two miles away. I even helped him move in.

Dave had already had a few attempts at killing Albert. He had planned to kill him in the Welsh cottage, but when he got there he lost his bottle. On Monday nights Albert used to go to see his old bandmaster in Knutsford, so Dave went there once or twice to kill him, but that did not work either. Another night he took my van on the by-pass and parked it, so it looked as if I had broken down, because Albert was supposed to be driving past. But Albert must have turned off earlier – anyway he did not stop.

The weekend before Albert died he was not well. I went round to his flat, cooked him something to eat and went back to my flat. We spent a night together. Then on the Tuesday Dave walked in and shot him dead.

That night Dave went off to play squash, then he was going to kill Albert. I met a friend and went with her to the pub. Albert had been to Salvation Army Band practice in Wrexham, which he did every Tuesday night. Dave sat and waited for Albert, with Albert's shotgun in his hands, and killed him when he came in through the door. Afterwards Dave came to the pub to tell me he had done it.

When I knew Albert was dead I just got pissed, so pissed I could not think. I felt completely empty about Dave. I never spoke to him after that night. Even when we were in custody and used to be taken to the court in the same transport I would not speak to him. I now feel nothing about him, I just feel sorry for him.

Albert was killed on Tuesday, 25 March, in the week leading up to Easter. The next morning they came for me and held me for four days before I confessed. Dave had said that if I said anything to the police he would get his organisation to injure my daughters. When I saw his statement, in which he confessed, I just told the police what had happened. By that time I was dead inside.

I was sent to Risley Remand Centre on Easter Saturday. I have never been so shocked in my life. There were women in blue dressing gowns effing and blinding. I wondered how I was ever going to survive. I was locked in a cubicle and told to take my clothes off and put on a dressing gown. When I came out they asked me what I was in for, and was it for children. I did not know what they were talking about, it was awful. It was terrible having to strip off in front of the women and then they went through my clothes, looking at the knickers I had just had on. They do it to humiliate you. It goes on here at Styall. One day I had been out shopping and when I got to reception the screw said I had to strip off. I told her I was having a period and she just handed me a clean sanitary towel. It nearly spoilt my day shopping but I refused to let it get to me.

When I first got to Risley I did not realise how dirty people could be because I hate being dirty and have to bathe regularly. I did not know what crabs were. When I started to itch I found crabs' eggs, but as I did not know what they were, I cleared them out myself by pulling them out.

The case was heard at Chester Crown Court a year later. It took twenty minutes because we both pleaded guilty. I have no idea what the judge said, but I was shocked when he said fifteen years. The screws in the remand centre had told me I was a model prisoner and I should be out in a couple of years. My solicitor just told me he knew as little about me at the end of the case as when he first met me. He could not understand me at all.

What I had done did not hit me until long after the trial.

I was sent to Durham Prison, which was absolutely horrendous. The sluices were overflowing and there was shit floating around.

I have done seven years and have eight to go. I am worried about becoming institutionalised and I fight against it. I refuse to play head games and I do not attend reviews, which stops me from having any chance of getting out early, but I will not become part of the system.

I think I should pay for what I have done – you cannot just go round arranging to knock off your husband – but I think another eight years is mad. The only thing now is that I might deteriorate – that is inevitable.

I am costing the country an awful lot of money; the only good thing is that I might come out with a degree.

I have come to terms with what I have done. People say that because I will not talk about it I am an enigma. I just do not like showing the screws my true feelings about it all, if I have any.

I did adore Albert. I loved and hated him. Everybody loved him except my daughters. He had a son and daughter of his own and he could be quite horrendous to them; there were periods when they did not speak. When his children came if they wanted anything from their Dad it was me they would come to, to work it out for them. He even sold his mother's house while she was still living in it.

I find it easy to talk about Albert and what happened because I did not do it. I have never seen him dead, I just remember him alive, with me. Looking back it all seems like a bad dream. I still long for Albert. I never think about Dave. I find Easter very difficult.

It has changed me. I am so strong now. No one could make me do anything. I would no longer be gullible or stupid.

Sinéad

Sinéad is under constant threat from Loyalist death squads in Belfast because she is married to a member of the IRA who has served sixteen years of a life sentence for killing two soldiers. She also works for the Republican cause herself. She did not tell me either her real name or where she lived. She chose the name Sinéad after the singer Sinéad O'Connor. I arranged the interview through Sinn Fein, who are not happy about an IRA man being part of a book about murderers. They say they spent years campaigning for their prisoners to have the status of political prisoners and that being seen in a criminal context puts the clock back. Sinéad, too, sees her husband as a soldier carrying out a necessary duty rather than murder.

However, I wanted to interview someone who fully supported what their loved one had done, and this can only be seen in someone who believes he or she is fighting for a cause.

Sinéad is in her mid-thirties, she is talkative, well educated and thoughtful – quite unlike the contrasting stereotypes of wild-eyed fanatic or downtrodden, ignorant wife left at home. She has spent her sixteen years without her husband, educating herself and campaigning for better conditions for Republican prisoners. She lives alone, waiting for him to be released from prison.

I had known Sean since I was about fifteen and we started going together when I was about seventeen. We both came from West Belfast. We got married when I was eighteen. That was basically what you did then; for most people of our age group that was part of growing up. Looking back on it now, it was just one of those cases where all my mates and I were going out together and we were pairing off with other mates who were going about together: it was a natural progression. I started dating and going to discos and then we started moving away from our friends and just the two of us were spending time together, going to the pictures and other places. It just happened naturally.

There was always something special about Sean: he was quieter than the rest of them, which was an attraction, and, I think, much more charitable towards women. In the culture we came from there was quite a lot of chauvinism in most of the men at that stage. He was different because he was always polite and very gentle, and I quite liked that. I also knew his family, so that helped as well.

This was 1977. Most people around here were political, and still are. We might not have classed ourselves as being political in those days, but we had an awareness from just living here, in a state which was being patrolled by armed soldiers and armed policemen. Most people were making political decisions about their lives every day. They were forced to do so. I knew he was a Republican – and I suppose I was too, to a degree – so I knew he was politically motivated, but I didn't know anything about his involvement with the Republican movement. I had no problems with that at all. It was just a natural way of going at that stage. It was fairly apparent there was a conflict – you only had to go out on to the streets to see the evidence of that: bombs going off, shootings, things like that, as a result of the British presence here. It was just something we all grew up with. I was about ten or eleven when it began in earnest.

Sean was two years older than me and had already left school to become an apprentice joiner when we met. I left school as soon as possible and worked in an office for a while until I got married.

I knew there was a distinct possibility that he was militarily active as well as being politically active. I thought he might be a member of the IRA because there were a number of tell-tale signs, like him being out at certain times but not being anywhere in particular. There was no big deal about that. It was never anything that I questioned him about, because I understood the reasons why he had to do it if he felt he wanted to do it. Perhaps I didn't want to know about it; perhaps I did not want to be faced with the prospect of the day-to-day living with fear. It is not a very nice thing to be sitting waiting for someone that you love thinking that he might be killed, shot, blown up or arrested. So I tried to push it to the back of my mind and I just tried to take it a day at a time. I also didn't want to know because if I knew, then the woman down the street would know what her husband was doing and then everybody would know. It is like any guerrilla warfare: the very essence of it is surprise, so you have to maintain a certain level of secrecy.

We had been married ten and a half months when Sean was arrested. It was around teatime and about five peelers [the RUC] came to the house where we lived. They knocked at the door, which was a common occurrence: we had been searched before and he had been arrested before, but he had never been charged. It was not unusual for me to get a knock on the door and for so many people to be waiting to come in and raid the house. I told them that Sean was not there and they just started laughing. They must have known that I didn't know what had happened at that stage. Normally I would have been watching the news at that time, but that evening, a Friday night, I wasn't. I think there was another programme I was watching. They didn't tell me that he had been arrested; they just came in and searched the house – by that I mean chiselling the bricks out of the fireplace, lifting the carpets and pulling up the floorboards, ripping open the back of the settee and searching all around there, looking in everything in the kitchen including pulling the cupboards off the wall and checking behind the wall. Upstairs in the bedroom, the wardrobe was turned upside down and the whole back was taken off. Lumps were cut out of the false wall so they could see into it. Sniffer dogs came in and they wet on the bedclothes. I could not claim any compensation because he had been arrested. It is terrifying, there is no doubt about it, it is absolutely terrifying. Then you have the invasion of privacy: they open your drawers and go through your underwear; your private letters are read. I heard them laughing and knew they were making jokes about it.

During all this my mother and his father came round to see what was going on. People must have told them that something was up. It was not as bad when they came because it was reassuring to have someone else with me. I was worried about leaving the house – not that I could have stopped the peelers from doing anything, but I did want to keep an eye on what they were doing. After they had left, someone came round and told me Sean had been arrested for shooting two soldiers dead.

I was devastated. I had a feeling of utter disbelief. I just thought it couldn't happen. While I wanted to know if he was all right, I felt that my whole life had just been turned upside down. It seemed that one minute we had been in our home together and now I did not know when he would ever return. I have to say that it had happened to a lot of people I knew, and I had been half expecting it. In the days that followed I found out how supportive the family and friends of our community can be.

I understood what he had done and why he had done it, although in the years to come I was to question it many times. I wanted to have children and I wanted us to be together, yet what he had done had prevented that; at the same time, I understood it and I still understand it. I support him.

When I first heard the news, as a natural self-preservation instinct I immediately worried about whether he was OK. It was only later that I thought about the people he killed. I thought about him killing two people. I thought about that quite often. I would be inhuman if I didn't think of them as two people: people who have families, perhaps wives, perhaps children. I try to put myself in their position. I don't think I have any real hatred or bitterness in me, but at the same time I understand why it has to happen. If you go back to the roots of the conflict and when the Six Counties State was set up in the 1920s, it has been a state that has been held by force: armed policemen and B specials. The Catholic minority was held down and oppressed in order to maintain the status quo and protect interests. In the sixties, all people wanted was basic civil rights, voting rights, housing – all the rights to which people are entitled. People on peaceful protests were beaten to the ground and shot dead. The IRA is a response to that type of oppression. You have to understand where those people who are members of the IRA come from and what they are used to. My husband had seen many of his friends shot down on the street; I have had many of my friends killed or arrested by the British army. I don't like killing of any description because I think you would have to be a psychopath to say you do not feel anything for those individuals who have been killed and their families, but everybody is a victim of this conflict and I don't think that any one community has suffered more than any other.

That was sixteen years ago, and even now, so many years down the road, the killing is still going on. Nobody in the British government has the courage to turn around and say: 'OK, let's stop this.' They are creating talks but they are not including the people who are going to help resolve the conflict within those talks. That is more frustrating than anything else now that they are still prepared, for whatever reasons, to allow it to continue for another 25 years. That is the part now that is really soul-destroying.

We rang round everywhere to find out what was happening. They could hold someone for seven days incommunicado, which they did eventually with Sean. We needed to get solicitors organised. The first couple of days there was so much to do that I just didn't have the time to sit and think about it. I was not even considering whether they would put him away for the rest of his life – all I was thinking about, at that stage, was getting things organised:

getting clothes ready to bring up to the interrogation centre, getting the solicitor ready to see him, basic things like that. The whole week was taken up in this way. It was a long week because I had no contact with him. The authorities were not compelled to allow a solicitor in after 48 hours, as they are now, so nobody was seeing him. I did not know what was happening, I just imagined he was in Castlereagh getting beaten. I was just totally disorientated. There were a few others arrested with him so I was milling around their families as well, talking to their partners and their wives, trying to find out wee bits and pieces about what was going on.

After four days we were notified that the solicitor had been in to see him. He said Sean was OK; he had had a beating but he was all right. The solicitor said he was going to be charged. When I asked him what he was going to be charged with he said it would be murder. We went down to Town Hall Street and were allowed in to have a visit with him the evening he was actually charged.

The first time, I saw him for about fifteen minutes, along with his mother and father. He was just trying to show us he was OK and that it was all right and I was not to worry about him. He was very concerned about me and how I was and did not talk about any worries about himself. I think that because Irish people have lived with so much death, destruction and devastation, we have learned to hide our fears and worries quite a bit. Some people might say we are very callous, but I think it is just a dignity. We are resigned to being dignified in our grief. Even people I have known who have lost relatives often do not appear to grieve, because we have learned to live with it for so long. My main concern was that he would not see me upset, even though I really was. I felt that would come later. I wanted him to go back to his cell feeling good about me. My main concern was about him, I hadn't the time to think about my own situation.

It was only in later years, when I sat and thought about it, that I would have all those different feelings of frustration and anger and whatever. It is then that it comes, not at the time; then I was able to truly explore my own feelings. He was worried about me and he was concerned about his family: his parents were not getting any younger. However, you have to remember that most of the people in our community are used to jails and jail life: you are always visiting people in jails whether they are cousins or brothers, uncles or aunts. I had several cousins in jail. So going to jail is not something that is unusual for members of our community.

The next morning Sean appeared in court, charged with murder. The night before a detective had gone and told him that he was being charged with murder and asked him if he had anything to say. He, like most people in that situation, said no. There was a magistrate in court who directed all his questions to the sergeant and the detective. He said: 'What did this person reply when he was charged?'

The detective said: 'No.'

That was taken as a not guilty plea. Later on in the trial the three of them dismissed their barristers and refused to recognise the court.

After that initial hearing Sean was sent to the Crumlin Road Prison and that afternoon I was allowed another visit. Remand prisoners are allowed three half-hour visits a week and I could take food parcels every time. That went on for just under two years. During that period I just seemed to be constantly running to the jail, because I had two of the visits every week while his family had the other one. I went on Monday and Friday and his family went in the middle of the week. Coming up to his trial I was taking all the visits.

I used to get up on a Monday morning and prepare everything for his food parcel ready for the visit that afternoon. Maybe I was lucky in that I had no children, because I used to see other women trailing three or four kids up to the prison. It was bad enough just trying to get myself and his parcel ready and get out to the Crumlin Road. It is not very far away but it is difficult to get to from West Belfast,

31

because you have to go into the town and get a bus up – no black taxis or anything go up there. Then I would come back on Monday evening and write a letter. That was my Monday.

I managed to get part-time work in a shop and worked on Tuesday mornings and Wednesday and Thursday evenings. Sean's family did his parcel on the Wednesday. They were very good. Then, on the Friday, there was the visit again. I would already have spent the Thursday getting ready for the visit on Friday, making up his food parcel. Then I would have the weekend and once that was over I would be back getting ready again for the Monday visit. So my life was very much dominated by prison, parcels and letters, and I did not get an awful lot of time to think about it.

Coming up to the trial I was aware of the Diplock court system, where one judge presides as judge and jury. Very few people went through it and came out the other end. Most people were convicted.

Their court case lasted two days, and the only reason it lasted that long was the deliberation of the prosecution. It was just a formality. I am not disputing that he did it, but if he had not I don't think he would have got off anyway. I have no faith in the British system of justice and the Diplock courts.

Sean was given two life sentences, which means they can hold him until the Secretary of State deems that he is fit to be released. He has served almost sixteen years. He is due for a review of his sentence when he has completed sixteen years, and we are waiting for that now. People do not put an awful lot of faith in it. The Review Board is not the same as the Review Board system in other countries. The prisoner is notified that he is up for review and he goes in and is asked questions at the Review Board. Then they go away and make a decision. There is no sort of representation on the prisoner's behalf, nor is there a solicitor present: there is nothing legal about it as such. It lasts maybe fifteen or twenty minutes. Several months later he is notified by the governor of the result. It is not a process where one is sitting biting one's nails waiting for it. Having said that it can be very trying for family members, because one wonders if this time they will refer him. They can give you a five-year knock-back, which means you are put back for another five years and you are not reviewed again until then; a four-, three-, two- or one-year knock-back, or they can refer you. Even if they say you are going to be referred, which means your papers go in front of the Secretary of State, he can give knock-backs, and has done so on occasions. So it is something that you are never sure of and at the time it is a wee bit nerve-racking. Coming up to it is not so bad, but about four months later when you get the result you feel a wee bit tense. Sean has already had a couple of knock-backs.

The sixteen years he has been inside have been very difficult at stages. It has been long at times. Sometimes I say, 'Sixteen years', and wonder if I have really been living through all this for that long. At the same time I am grateful that I am able to visit him – at least he is not dead. Then another part of me wonders if I have wasted my life, and what is going to happen when he gets out for good. Is it going to be the same?

We have been together alone during that time because he has been out on parole. When he reached thirteen years he was allowed to come out for a week twice a year, at Christmas and in the summer, so he has been in and out on parole seven times now. Getting used to that each time was tough.

The first time was like a second honeymoon. It was really brilliant. For the months coming up to it I got all prepared. I had the flat done up and everything sorted out for him; everything was new. It was great. Then he had to go back. I was up on a merry-go-round and the next thing I was down on the ground again. It was very, very hard coping with it.

The second time was a bit similar but I did not feel quite as bad when he went back in. The third time was the worst, because it was almost 'here we go again'. By the time I had come to the third parole I had reached the stage where the curtains were not being changed any more, nothing new was being bought for the house because the money just was not there. I kept thinking how I would feel when he went back; the whole week was overshadowed by that feeling. He normally takes Friday to Friday and on about the Tuesday or the Wednesday I would say to myself: 'Oh no. It is only a couple of days before I'll feel like that again.' But as the visits go on they seem to get a bit easier.

No matter how much time passes I think the uncertainty of the life sentence has a big effect on my psychological self. I never know when he will be back; one day he could just walk in the door. I certainly wonder what it is going to be like when he is back here for good.

I have changed tremendously. I have gone from being the young naïve girl I was when I first met him to someone who is fairly independent. I have become used to my independence: I have built a home of my own, and everything in my home has been chosen by me.

I have seen an awful lot of change in Sean as well. He was always charitable towards women but now he has a tendency to go overboard. In the prison they do all these childcare courses and women's studies and different things like that. Whilst I welcome that, and I welcome the fact that they are prepared to open their minds to those type of issues, at the same time it is all theory, because he is living in an all-male environment. Putting it to practical use out here is not just a matter of him going in and doing the dishes or trying to be feminist-minded – there is a lot more to it than that, things like sharing decision-making.

That is where we have our biggest problem. He cannot understand how I have changed. He will say: 'Let's sit down and talk about this.' But at the end of the day he thinks we should abide by what he decides. He can not understand that I have been making decisions about my life for so long, that I almost resent this person coming back into my life and saying: 'Do you not think it would be better doing it this way?'

There are difficulties there, but they are not major. I think any people living together, particularly a couple who have been apart for several years – and I know that the length of time that we have been apart is a lot longer than most – are going to have problems. But I think getting used to somebody again is going to be very difficult.

On top of that we have the whole thing of children. Do we start a family now? We are caught up in all those decisions that we have to make too. How do we feel about that? How is it going to fit into my life now? I have been back to college – how is that all going to fit in? I think children have to be my decision and not a joint decision because it affects my life more than it affects his. He is liable to go back and do what he wants to do and I am going to be left with the baby. Typical Irish culture: the mother is home and the father is out, so the responsibility for the children is left in the hands of the mother. The first few times he came out on parole we deliberately did not allow me to get pregnant; now we are just leaving it to chance. It is not a big chance – two weeks out of a year – so I don't feel threatened by that in any way. I don't know how I would feel if I found myself pregnant; at the same time I know that I am not getting any younger. I know that it is going to have to come some time. I don't want to have my first baby too late; even becoming pregnant is more difficult at that stage.

It is not as if we have this magical love affair that has come through fifteen years. We have actually separated several times. On one occasion we separated for a year and a half because I said that I was not prepared to spend my whole life like this. I was 26 at the time and I didn't feel that I could cope with living my life around a man in jail any more. There is a lot of pressure round here and I just could not accept being a prisoner's wife. I wanted out of it. I wanted to go out with other people. Looking back on it now, I do not know if I knew what I wanted, I just wanted out. It was like an entrapment and that was the way I felt.

It was not that one day I just decided that I wanted out; it grew over a period of time. We were having bad visits. In all it was a period of about three years – the separation was almost two years but the whole build-up to it and the aftermath was a lot longer. I found I had to disregard the pressure from the community and stop thinking about what other people thought about me and get on with my life. It is like most communities: people gossip, but at the end of the day if you want to make a decision about your life and you have courage enough to do it you should go through with it. I did not want to go on seeing him, so I told him and I led a fairly separate life from him. I meant it to be final. However, he was always in the background and I was always wondering how he was. I found that I was not fulfilled outside the relationship. I was just as miserable outside it as I was inside it. I don't think I have ever stopped loving him. I am not saying that that has kept us together, but it gives me hope for the future. I don't believe love is enough to keep us together. I think we need more than that.

There is a sense of fulfilment even though he is not here. The fact that I know Sean is going to be here at some stage makes a difference. Seeing him makes a difference, even if it is just one visit a week now they are sentenced – even if the contact is just through letters – there is still that shared emotion and that shared feeling. He is a very helpful type of a person. If I am having problems he can sit and talk to me about them.

That was the main reason I went back, because I could never see me getting involved in a serious relationship with anyone else.

I don't think it does any harm to have those separations because we have coped fairly well. All in all, the very fact that we are still together after all that time, even though there were separation periods, shows we have stood the test of time. But I don't think I will know for certain whether I can live with him until he is out for good. That is when it will become clear. But I know I will definitely not leave him before then. I am prepared to wait to take my chance, and if it is the case that we have grown apart too much we are going to have to make a decision about what we are going to do. But I would not feel it was wasted time, either. I am going to have to say to myself that I could have been with him for all those years and still at the end of it feel unfulfilled and want to leave, so it is something I have to go through.

I do not see what he did as a crime and I do not see him as a criminal as such. I think what he did has not so much made me more political as channelled the politicisation that I did have into a certain area, in the sense that I have been active in the lifers' campaign and in jail-related issues. But I would always have seen myself as being fairly politically minded, anyway. It is a natural thing for anybody from the community that I come from.

However, I have chosen not to be a member of the IRA. That is a personal choice, because I just do not believe I would be able to go to prison and I do not think I would be prepared to risk my life. I am not ashamed to say that. I don't think I would be prepared to make the sacrifices that he was prepared to make. Although it has been difficult for me and it has affected me, I am still out here and he is the one who is locked up. I would not have taken the decision to join the IRA and end up doing sixteen years or more in prison, although I admire anybody who does.

I don't think I could kill people. Personally, I do not believe I could but at the same time I know the type of person Sean is and I know that he is not capable of killing just for killing's sake, either. It is a case where he, like most people in the Republican movement and the IRA, could not see any other way. This type of conflict has been forced on them. It is not a decision which they have taken lightly. Nobody takes a decision to join the IRA lightly, because most people I have known who have been in the IRA have either ended up doing long, long years in prison or else are dead: young people with their whole lives in front of them, young people who have left behind widows and small children. So it is not a decision that anybody takes lightly. To me it is a decision that you sit back and think about. Even if you are politically motivated it is not the natural thing to just go out and join the IRA. It is natural to want to do it – the British try to paint the picture that the IRA are not normal people, and they certainly are normal people – but I think you have to be prepared to make those sacrifices. That is the type of individual you have to be.

I don't know what I would have thought if it had been a bombing like Warrington, which killed children, rather than two soldiers who were killed. I have tried to put myself in the position of those soldiers' wives or families; sometimes I even wonder what their wives feel about me. I know that I am speaking for most relatives of people who have been in prison for things like that; the men in prison are not psychopaths and they are not people who do that sort of thing lightly. Everybody must have been moved by the death of those children in Warrington, especially that young one – anybody who was not moved by that must be totally inhuman – but I think the point was missed: people here have suffered that way for years. I know families who have lost children as young as that young boy; I know families who have lost children out playing in the streets, shot dead by plastic bullets where there has been no riot. Our children have been killed too.

If Sean had killed a child by mistake, obviously it may have been a wee bit more difficult for me. But I would have recognised that it was not a deliberate act and that he did not set out to kill the child. The longer this conflict goes on the more and more people are going to die in it. Death is something that has touched us all.

When Sean was first in jail I did feel frustrated and resentful. Everybody wants something out of life and we all have a tendency to personalise it. I used to ask myself, what have I got here? And the answer was: absolutely nothing. I would get angry that my life was revolving around a prison visit once a week in Long Kesh. When problems arose, like financial difficulties, because I had a home to run and there were all sorts of troubles, or maybe I was just feeling tense and depressed and down, I would think, he is not here and he should be here to help me.

But I learned that I had to deal with all those angry feelings and depressions. In the beginning I would bottle them up and I did not allow myself to express them. When I was with Sean, I was constantly biting my tongue and pretending everything was OK when it was not. It was only when I reached the stage of being angry and I was sitting and talking about my anger that I began doing something constructive about it. I went to quite a number of women's awareness classes, so I was lucky enough to be able to articulate those feelings of anger. I think I would have been more constrained if I had had children, but because I was very much on my own with good family support and friends, I was able to go out with them and I was able to go to these places.

I look around me here, in this community, and there are so many unhappy women, even those in relationships where their partners are there, and that awareness has come out of my education. It has allowed me to say: 'OK, my situation is bad, but I would not swap it with the woman down the road, who is getting battered every weekend when her husband comes home with too much drink in him. Or another woman whose husband is being unfaithful, and who is being humiliated.'

So that sense of anger is in a lot of them. I try to focus it saying: 'Well, it would not be all rosy in the garden if he was here, either. He would probably have turned out like the rest of them.'

You have to work at being happy. While I could never say I was really happy, I think reasonably content is what you aim for. If you have got a certain degree of contentment in your life and a certain amount of fulfilment I think that that is all you can hope for.

In this situation it is all you can hope for, because you face a threat from so many different people. I face a threat from the RUC and the British army, but I also face a threat from Loyalist death squads. You do not have to be a member of the IRA to be shot dead by them. They shot dead two kids who were serving in a mobile shop, fifteen and sixteen years old. Relatives of prisoners have been shot before. It is a constant threat, and I will be more worried about it when he comes out; I worry about it when he is out on parole, too.

Watching oneself all the time is a natural thing. It is nothing abnormal for people who live in the Republican community. We have to have security in the house for a start; we have to have a heavy door. I am always conscious of noises in the night when I am lying in bed. I am conscious when I go outside my own area with Sean. Will anybody recognise him? Would anybody recognise me when I visit him? I am always looking to see if there is somebody suspicious-looking on the street. It is just a natural part of coming from the Republican community. You have to be very vigilant and cautious. It has saved people's lives before.

I sometimes wonder what my life would have been like if Sean had not gone into prison. It is more than likely that I would have had three or four children by now, because we had talked about having kids. Most of my mates had three or four children by the time they were 25, so it would have been quite natural for me to have followed that pattern. In that respect I think my independence would not have come to the surface so much because I would have had to care for my children and wait for them to be grown before I could have attended all these classes.

In the beginning I found it difficult saying to myself: 'Right! You go and set yourself goals.' Because I was used to Sean being part of my life and making decisions it was difficult, although I have to say I adapted fairly quickly to it and I actually liked it. I enjoy the sense of independence, which I would never have achieved if I had had children because there would have been other family constraints on me like financial responsibility. Now my money is my own. OK, I have electricity bills and house bills and I am still having to look after the clothes and stuff, but at least I have money for myself to spend in the way I want to spend it. I think it is very important to be financially independent, then going a step further and broadening the horizons through education. Education has been the biggest factor in my own self-awareness.

My education has been fairly informal. I have done several university courses, not at Queen's [a Belfast university] but at a technical college. I have done quite a lot of courses on women's studies. I started it all by reading about an assertiveness course. I went on that and it took me into psychology a little bit more, and I did a few short twelve-week courses. Then I took a couple of full-time courses during the day, and I met some very interesting people through that. I found it very mentally stimulating. I did not only meet people like myself: I have been to London once and the thing that struck me was the different cultures. Here you might socialise for years and you would never meet anybody outside your own community. That really oppressed me. I got to the stage where I wanted to break out of that mould. I did not want to be always stuck with the same type of people who thought the same way. People on the courses had all shades of opinion and I found that very interesting. When you come from a small, narrow culture like ours you can have a tendency to become totally engrossed in it and for it to be so all-enveloping that you feel that there is nothing else outside it. I feel that it is a good thing to see other cultures and to travel and see how other people live. London really was impressive. I loved it when I went over there, even though it was only for two weeks. I remember one evening in particular: it was a women's meeting, and there were Palestinian women, Islamic women, Jewish women, all working to their own different agendas in terms of their own culture, but they also had one common agenda because they were all oppressed as women. That was the central theme of the meeting. It was great, listening to all the different viewpoints and all the different people. It was an informal session, we were all sitting round drinking wine and eating cheese, and I had never been used to anything like that before and found it very stimulating.

When I look back to when I was sixteen and seventeen I have changed, but I am still constrained. Living here constrains me day to day because I am so limited in the places I can go and the type of people I can meet. But at the same time I have changed because I want more out of life. Sean is very supportive of how I have changed. When I came back from London I was full of it. I went to visit him and told him he had to go to London. He just looked at me slightly disbelievingly and said: 'Yeah, I'll go to London.' He has studied a few women's courses and different things – academically he would probably outshine me because he has had excellent results – but he has still no practical experience. I would hope that maybe in later years, once the conflict is over, we would travel a bit and see other people's cultures.

I am plagued by the question of whether I would want him to leave the IRA when he comes out. I do not know. I don't know how I would feel if he went back to jail again. I most certainly do not believe I will go back and see him again for all those years. But at the same time, although my own consciousness has been raised by all those other issues concerning women, I have to allow for him to make his own decisions too. Obviously in conjunction with me, because it affects my life as well. It is something we are going to have to sit down and discuss. At the same time he has spent the last sixteen years of his life in prison for something close to his heart, so I don't know how he would feel about leaving. He can hardly just turn his back on it. It would be very difficult to do that. However, it is impossible to be in the IRA and not have the threat of prison hanging over you and not to be prepared for the consequences. Anybody who is in the IRA who thinks that they are not going back to jail or that they are not going to be dead one day is living in fairyland. You only have to look at the figures for people who have been shot dead and have been in prison to bear that out. I know people who have spent long years in jail and have come out here and been killed, so the threat is always there. You are never going to live without that threat if you do decide to go back. But we will leave the decision until he gets out for good. We'll discuss it then.

One thing about our community is that it is very supportive, and if you have a problem you can go and talk to friends and relatives about it. It is probably a major factor in why I have managed to stay with Sean. The fact that the Republican community has an inherent respect for prisoners helps to make sure wives are not isolated. Their prisoners are well looked after and are respected. Everybody here really goes out of their way, particularly throughout the prison protests, when prisoners went 'on the blanket'. They wore only blankets, refusing to put on prison uniform because they said they were political prisoners and not criminals. Then the women and relatives walked the streets for years. They went all over the world speaking about their sons and their relatives who were on the protest. There is an awful lot of political support among families and relatives and friends – that is a major plus, because I could not even attempt to draw a comparison between me and someone whose husband has been given a life sentence for other things. A woman like that would probably be isolated from her community, especially if it was a fairly horrific crime, as happened to Sonia Sutcliffe, Peter Sutcliffe's wife. I don't think it was fair taking it out on his wife. Whatever you feel about what he did, his wife had nothing to do with it. Yet she was persecuted by the press and the public. I don't know if I could withstand that type of pressure. I don't believe I could.

Sean was one of the men who went 'on the blanket'. Even now, thinking about it, I can't come to terms with it. He was on it for two years, and what it meant was that he was living in a cell six feet by four feet and he had no clothing at all, just a blanket for protection. He was forced on to a no-wash protest, because in order to go out to use

43

the showers he had to put on prison uniform. So he refused to shower, and he had to go to the toilet in his cell and spread it all over the walls. The reason he did that was because it was the only way to dry it out and stop it from smelling; so that it would not just be lying in the cell. He was not shaving so he had a beard and grew his hair long. I don't think anybody who did not see those men at the time could appreciate the horrendous conditions they were living in. They were just skeletons. Sean went down to something like ten stone and he is a big man, broad and tall. In those days there was a visit once a month. The screws were totally hostile during the visits and I very rarely got a visit on my own. There was a period where I didn't see him for eight months, when the men were refusing visits, again because in order to take visits they had to put on a prison uniform. The screws used to look at the men, and if they were tall and broad they used to give them wee uniforms, so that the trousers were way up their legs and the jackets did not fit, and if they were small they would give them big ones. They were that vindictive. The men used to come out with these 'mobby suits', as we called them, and the smell on them was unbelievable. They would sit at one side of the table and you would have to sit at the other. There was no physical contact at all. You had a hostile screw standing over you.

To be honest I don't know even to this day how I went up to see him like that. It really was very difficult going up, even to watch him. It used to break my heart. That was one of the most trying periods of the whole imprisonment. It was really dreadful. Conditions have changed so much since then. You would hardly know the place. Even visiting conditions have changed so much for the better. There is a more personable atmosphere among the screws, almost a friendly type of atmosphere. I find that there is not so much hostility. Perhaps there are one or two bad ones, but on the whole it is not as bad. It makes a lot of difference, even though he is still being held in jail. I can actually enjoy my visits now.

I always got on well with Sean's parents, even before I was going out with him. I lived a couple of streets away from them. I never had any problems with them and even during the time that we were separated they never treated me any different. They still came round to visit me and they told me they understood what was going on. I was one of the lucky ones, because not everybody had that type of atmosphere. My parents and Sean's were friends so we never had a problem. I always had a great relationship with them, apart from being his wife.

They try to keep a happy-go-lucky type of outlook. They talk about the review when he has done his sixteen years and they say: 'Maybe with the help of God.'

They are very religious people, too, his mother especially. She says: 'I will do that novena and I will do this novena.'

I sit there trying to tell them not to build their hopes up. There is a strong possibility that he will get a one-year knock-back, or maybe even a two-year knock-back. But it is hard not to build up expectations, even if you know the system; it is hard not to have that wee bit of hope. He has had knock-backs before, a three-year and then a two-year knock-back. It is something we are going to have to come to terms with if and when it happens.

It has affected my life quite a bit. It would have been totally different if he had been one of those people who, when we got married, went to work in the mornings and came home from work in the evenings. By now we probably would have had a mortgage, a house of our own, children and all those things that maybe you used to want. There has been a definite lack of material things, but I think there have also been plusses: because he has been through jail he is probably a lot more committed and determined than he was before. That has also affected me to a degree because it has made me look at things. When you are growing up with something and it is always round you it is just a natural progression to go from one thing to another and become more involved. I think that the whole political side of things has made me more aware of what is actually going on in the likes of the Diplock courts. I had heard of it, but actually being a victim of it is a totally different thing. Going through the jail protests and the prison visits has made me a stronger person and has also given me an awareness in that I have opened my mind to other areas of life. That has helped me to understand people better and understand myself better. It gives you a better tolerance of people and other people's cultures.

Andrea Aitken

I did not want this book to concern only 'criminals', but also killing which is considered acceptable by society, like that of soldiers. The Trauma After Care Trust specialises in dealing with the terrible after-effects suffered by men involved in battle, who may have killed or had friends killed near them. The Trust also helps to deal with the pain inflicted on their families. They put me in touch with Andrea. When I spoke to her on the telephone, she was happy to tell me of the effect that her husband Tony's two years with the Welsh Guards in Northern Ireland had on him.

He was on patrol one day when the man in front of him was blown up by a landmine. In a later incident he killed someone. Andrea and I arranged to meet.

A few days later Tony rang me to say that she did not know anything about his time in Ireland, so perhaps I should talk to him. I explained that the book was about the women involved with the men, and it didn't matter that she didn't know very much about what happened because he never talked about it. I was slightly perplexed, because she had described to me exactly what had happened to him. The day before Andrea and I were due to meet Tony rang me to say that Andrea had had a bad asthma attack and was in hospital, so she could not see me. When we finally met he admitted that he had stopped the interview because he did not trust me. However, after he checked me out he allowed Andrea to be interviewed. I have no idea how I was checked out.

We met in the lounge of a Cardiff hotel. Tony escorted Andrea and sat with us throughout the interview. As she

47

catalogued his appalling behaviour he nodded, almost proud-
ly. Only once did he stop her. She was telling me how abusive
he was when drunk and he pointed out that he had never laid
a finger on her or their two children. She agreed with him
and then went on to tell me how dreadful he was in every
other way.

He is obsessed, nearly twenty years after leaving Northern
Ireland, with security measures. Taxis must always pick him
up and drop him off away from his home so no one discovers
his address. He comes in over the back fence so no one knows
when he returns to the house. He made it clear to me that he
knew what 'really went on' in Northern Ireland, particularly
covert operations and collusion between the security services
and the outlawed Protestants.

Andrea is a very attractive, blonde woman whose appear-
ance belies her massive insecurity. She seems spirited and
self-possessed, yet is dependent on her husband. She has
chronic asthma which is so disabling that she can no longer
work. The family live in a Cardiff suburb.

I met Tony when I was eighteen. I was unemployed and
living in a small town in South Wales. He had a big dealer-
ship selling cars and a man I used to go out with told him
that I was looking for a job. He rang me up and asked me
to come immediately for an interview to be his secretary. I
did, and he offered me the job there and then. I began
straight away.

After I started working for him, he just kept chasing me.
He kept sitting in my office, trying to get me to go out with
him, but I didn't want to know. I was seeing someone at
the time and I didn't want to go out with anyone else, but
he kept on and on and on. In the end I said: 'All right then,
anything for a quiet life.'

He took me out to Cardiff one evening and that was it.
Within three months we were engaged. I don't know why
I fell for Tony. He just seemed nice to be with and fun.

He didn't tell me he had been a soldier in Northern Ireland until after we were married. We were packing up to

move house and I found some memento I had not seen before, I forget exactly what it was. He told me he had had it when he was in the army. I just thought it was all part of his past, which was over with, and moved on to talk of other things. How wrong I was!

The first inkling that he had a problem came before we got married when he went to Spain. My sister came to stay at my house with me. I had a phone call from Tony saying he was not coming back and that I should cancel the wedding. Then he put the phone down on me and there was no way I could contact him. I was devastated. I didn't know what to do. He was due home the following day so, on the off-chance, I went to the airport to meet him off the plane. He came through arrivals and greeted me as if nothing had happened. I told him what he had said over the phone and he did not remember any of it. He just asked me what I was talking about.

Then a month before we were married he went back to Spain to look at a boat and he did it all again. He rang me the night before he was due to come home to tell me he was not coming back and did not want to marry me. Again he told me that I should cancel the wedding. I went to the airport again and, as before, he said hello as if nothing had happened while he had been away. He just did not remember. I didn't know what to think.

I thought something was wrong after we got married because he started drinking a lot. Before we married he was fine, and we used to go everywhere together. However, three months later I fell pregnant and I used to stay in. He would go out alone and roll home drunk. Sometimes he would go off for days at a time. I could not figure out what was wrong. At first I just thought he liked his beer. My father always liked a drink, but he would go down to the pub at eight and come home at eleven. Tony went out at eleven and came home when he had run out of money, which might be at two in the morning or days later.

When he goes out in the morning, I don't know when I am going to see him again: it could be an hour or two or three days. Quite often I will have gone to bed and at about two in the morning I will get a phone call from the police to say that he has been locked up for drink-driving and they will release him in the morning.

When he has been gone for the night, he comes back in as if he has only popped out for five minutes. He just walks in and says: 'All right?' Then he goes out and starts shouting at the neighbours. They do not see him the next day, so I get all the funny looks. They don't say anything, it is just the whispers and looks, but they stop their children playing with ours and that hurts. I say to him: 'You can't keep doing this, not when it's affecting them. You have to stop it.'

Our problems with the neighbours have got so bad that several times we have had to move house. We can't go on doing that to the children.

Tony can be lovely when he's sober, but I don't like him when he has been drinking. When he comes home he often says some really hurtful things, but when I mention it the next morning he doesn't remember any of it. Before we had the children, I used to walk out because I couldn't take it. It was easier just to go. Otherwise I would just start an argument and he would start hitting the doors, calling me names and smashing things. He is not as bad as he used to be but that is because I know not to wind him up when he is drunk. He has never lifted a finger to me or the children.

We don't drink together because I have given up alcohol. He drinks enough for the two of us. I don't go out very often anyway, because of the children.

I have thought about leaving him plenty of times but then the next day, when he is sober, he can be lovely. I ask him why he drinks if it is going to get him in that state and he says he will stop. He may stop drinking or going out for weeks, but then it starts all over again. It is only then that I think, I don't want this and I cannot go on living like it. He is so nice when he is sober that it makes me think that this is the real person. If the children were not there I would go when he gets drunk, but I can't keep waking them up to dress them and take them to my mother's. So I wait until morning. By then he is so nice that I think, oh well, I'll give him another chance.

The children don't know what to make of him. They can come in one day and he is as nice as pie, but if he has had a drink he just doesn't want to know them. They don't know where they stand and nor do I half the time. It isn't easy living with him. It is very hard explaining to the children why he is like he is. They ask me: 'Why is Daddy shouting at me when I haven't done anything?' He is very short-tempered.

Tony has been married three times. His mother said that he used to have the moods and drink during his first two marriages and neither wife could stick him, either. I don't know much about his first wife, but he says he married the second, Linda, because his father wanted to see him settled down. When his father died he left her.

When I first tried to question him about his drinking, he dismissed it, saying that I didn't really know what was going on because I come from a little village where men don't really drink. His friends from Cardiff seemed exactly the same, so I just thought that was how Cardiff people behaved. But then his friends started to ring up and say he had smashed up a pub or something, and they don't behave like that. So I realised he was different from them. He wouldn't think twice about smashing up a pub or causing a fight in the middle of one. He will just drink himself silly. His friends try to put him in a car and send him home, but when he has had a drink, he will not listen to anybody.

It is not just his drinking that worries me. He doesn't seem able to stick at anything. He built up two successful businesses – car sales and a nightclub – but then he got bored and let other people run them. Of course, now they have both gone bust.

With the nightclub he signed the house away. He got me to sign something. I didn't know what I was signing and now I have found out that it involves the house. There was no legal representation and I had just come out of hospital after one of my asthma attacks, so all I wanted to do was sign and get out. I just trusted him too much, although I am not sure he really understood what it meant either. Now it looks as if we might lose the house because they are still trying to repossess it. I worry about it all the time, but nothing bothers him. He just says, 'Never mind.'

He was arrested for credit card fraud at Christmas and I am worried he will go to jail. He just says he probably won't and he can handle it if he does.

He doesn't trust me at all. He tries not to let me speak to anyone. If I go to the doctor's, he insists on coming in with me. Whatever I do, he is there. When I come back from somewhere on my own he will ask where I have been, who I talked to and what I said. He is jealous. He doesn't like me talking to anybody. I went out with the girls the other night and before I went I had a list of dos and don'ts: don't talk to any of the fellas, don't have drinks off anybody. I said, 'For God's sake, I'm only going out!'

When I came home I got: 'Who did you see? What did you say?'

I just said: 'I won't go out again, because you just want to know the ins and outs of everything.'

He thinks everybody is talking about him but it isn't true. He is afraid of what people might think about him but they are not interested. It is all in his head. He had an argument with the neighbour across the road one day. That night he came in about midnight and went over there with a knife and slashed the tyres on their car because of the argument. He is just crazy. The neighbour didn't say anything, but he knew who it was. Now they even talk to each other. When he is in that mood I have to watch him, because I just don't know what he will do.

When we lived in Cardiff, we had a field at the back of the house. When he came home, he used to black up his face and come through the back of the field because he didn't want the taxi driver to know where we lived. We had a six-foot fence up at the back so he would climb over that. He would never let a taxi drop him off outside the house or pick him up from the house: he would always arrange to meet them at the end of the road. It sounds crazy, but I have learned to live with it.

When he is drunk he talks about what happened to him in Northern Ireland. He goes on and on about it. But the rest of the time he never talks about it. He was on patrol one day, with three other soldiers, and the man in front of him stepped on a landmine and was blown up. He also shot some people. He always tells me that I don't understand what it was like. He says I don't understand how it feels to have your friend blown up in front of you. He has talked to me about shooting people; he is not certain if he hit them, but he probably did. When I asked him how he felt about that, he just said it did not bother him.

He gets obsessed with Northern Ireland when he has had a drink. He will shout at me: 'You don't know what it's like to kill somebody.'

I say: 'I know I don't. I've never done it.'

I am not saying that I do understand, but there is no need to keep going on about it. I would rather not know about what he has done. The less I know, the less I have to think about. I have done my best. I have tried to understand. I have sat down and listened, but whatever I say it is always the same; he says: 'See? You never listen and you don't understand.' It is easier to shut up.

I don't really know how he feels about the times in Northern Ireland. I think a lot about the man who was killed on patrol and even more about the other two who were there, who have since killed themselves. He is the only one left. It makes me wonder if he is going to do something stupid like that. I hope he is not that stupid, but when he goes missing for days on end I just don't know what he is doing. It makes me wonder what he would do if he thought about killing himself when he was drunk, because if someone told him to jump off the cliff, he would. He wouldn't think of the danger, he would just do it. He has climbed over walls and come home with burns all up his arms just because people have told him to do it. At other times I have had to take him up to the hospital for stitches because he has been fighting. I would hate to see him in the army again because if he is still like he is now, he would shoot at anything that moves.

When I asked him what he thought about shooting people he said that he didn't think about it. It was just a job he had to do. But I couldn't do it. He says it doesn't bother him that he had to kill and injure people; he says the way he looks at it, it was either him or them. What happened to him in Northern Ireland has ruined my life.

I don't like to think that he has killed someone but there is nothing I can do about it, so I just have to try to accept it. I met Tony ten years after he came out of the army so I only get bits of the story, and some of that from his mother and brothers. His mother could see the change in him and she also hates it when he has had a drink, because when he comes home he rings everybody – it doesn't matter what time it is, he just rings. If he has got your number he will ring you. His mum says that if he has been drinking she doesn't want to know because he is horrible; she has asked him not to ring her. One day he rang her at three o'clock in the morning just to say hello and she knew straight away that he had had a drink because he started calling everyone in the family names. Now she will not answer the telephone if it is late at night because she knows that it will be him.

He also rings my mother, but she just laughs at him. She thinks he is funny. She says: 'Tony, put the phone down and I'll speak to you in the morning.' Other people get nasty with him and I try and tell him not to ring anyone.

One day I bought the paper, the *Wales on Sunday*, and there was an article about all these soldiers who had been in the Falklands, what they had done there and how it had affected them since. I told Tony the article could have been written about him because their behaviour was so similar. There was a telephone number at the bottom to ring for the Trauma After Care Trust, a charity which deals with people who have been soldiers. Tony rang it and Doug

Morris came down the next day to see him. Doug said Tony was suffering from a classic case of post-traumatic stress disorder, and that his drinking bouts and other behaviour problems were symptoms of it. Then Tony went to see a psychologist and she said that he was 90 per cent traumatised and that he needed treatment for it.

The trauma people say they can do something about it, and I am sure they will. The problem is that to get treatment he has to go to East Grinstead in Surrey for seven days and we have to find the money for him to stay somewhere and to pay for the treatment. At the moment we just do not have the money to do that because he is out of work. Until he starts earning I have to put up with his behaviour or tell him to go, but I don't want to do that. Wendy, Doug Morris's wife, says that what I feel is quite common. I rang her up crying the other day because he had phoned me and said that he wanted a divorce. He said he didn't want to see me or the children and that I had tricked him into having children. When I told Wendy, who tends to deal with the wives of the traumatised soldiers, she said that she gets this about nine or ten times a week. She said that it is very common and the men have to have treatment for it. He needs about 40 hours' treatment, and Doug says that he should stop drinking, but until then we don't know whether it will work.

When he is asleep he shouts out and gets me out of bed because he is dreaming that he is shooting or chasing somebody. It is always to do with Northern Ireland. Doug and Wendy are convinced that he is trying to deal with what happened to him when he was there. Whatever he says, killing somebody does bother him. They say they are all classic symptoms of post-traumatic stress. I don't understand it at all. I just want him to go for treatment and hopefully then he will be all right – although sometimes I don't think he will ever be all right.

He is now supposed to stop drinking, but he hasn't. He is supposed to have done lots of things to help himself, but it is only after he has been drinking that he thinks, Oh, I shouldn't have done that. Then he will stop for a week or two, but he always goes back to it.

It is not easy to live with him even though I now know what is wrong with him. I get up some days and I hate him. I tell him I hate him and that I want him to go. I don't mean it, I don't want him to go; it is just that probably he has said some really horrible things through drink the night before and they still hurt. He doesn't understand that, so I think I would be better off if he went. Sometimes when he is away, I think that I can't stand waiting about the house wondering if he is going to come home; then if he does come home, wondering what sort of mood he will be in and whether he will be sober or drunk and whether he will start screaming and shouting at me. If he comes in sober he will be all over me, telling me how much he loves me, yet at other times I hate him. I have run away from the house before to get out and he has stood out in the street screaming, telling me to come back.

As the years have gone on, he has got worse. The drinking binges are longer and the moods are blacker. He gets very moody very often: one minute he can be really nice but the next he is shouting and screaming at me.

I know why he is like he is, I just wish he wasn't. I just wish they could do something.

It was all wonderful when we got married but then he changed. His brothers have told me that he has been like this since he joined the army. When we met he was probably trying to impress me, so I did not see that side of him. When we started living together and the children came along, I could see him changing. It is worse than it has ever been because he drinks so much. When I first met him, he had been told to give up the drink because he only had six months to live. But he just will not listen to anybody. He has changed so much since I married him that it is like being married to somebody else.

At first, when he used to come in and say: 'I don't remember ringing you,' I would wonder if he was winding me up. At least I know now why he does things like that, but it still upsets me a lot. When he says all these awful things it is like someone sticking a knife into me. I cannot forget what he says, but when I bring it up the next morning he just replies: 'Haven't you forgiven me yet?' I can't forgive him so easily because I remember all the little things he has said to me, all the things that have hurt.

I am still with him because when he is not drunk he is lovely and there are more times when he is not drunk. But when he is drunk I hate him and I think, I cannot take this any more. But when he is sober he will say: 'Come on, we'll go here,' or 'Let's take the kids there.' Then I think, Perhaps he is not so bad after all. I hope it will all go away with this treatment because they say that it *can* be treated; they say that they have treated hundreds of people. I just wish he was one of the hundreds.

One night I was on the phone for over an hour talking to Wendy because I was so upset. Tony had rung up, saying: 'I want you and the children out of the house before I get home. I want a divorce.' When I rang Wendy she told me to sit tight and he would come home. She said: 'You have put up with this for nine years, so you should know what he is like by now. I know it's easy for me to say he'll be home, but he will.' An hour later he walked in through the door, and he did not even remember ringing me.

Tony says that he doesn't mean what he says, but why say it? He just turns round and says: 'You know what I am like when I've had a drink.' At one time we were having really bad arguments so I packed his bags and told him to go. I didn't want him to go but he had been saying hurtful things to me so I thought I would get back at him.

I know I shouldn't listen to anything he says but I do. Wendy tells me to hang on in there. She says that once he has had his treatment it will be like living with a different person.

After the explosion in Northern Ireland he didn't have any treatment, he just went straight back on patrol. Of course he should have been taken off patrol, and talked to about what had happened. The man behind was killed outright and when he went to cover the wound he found that his hand had gone straight through the man's stomach. Something like that is bound to affect him, but he was never given any treatment or advice or anything. It is on his mind all the time and he cannot forget. He needs to be taught how to forget it all and to let it go, but he just bottles things up. For instance, he still has his army jacket in the house. Doug told him to get rid of it but he refuses to. He also has his army bag, which he won't throw out either. Doug says that if he gets rid of them it will be one less thing to remind him about what happened. I have decided that after the treatment it all has to go. At the moment we are just waiting for the treatment and I hope the man I fell in love with will come back and we can be married again. Perhaps that man will never return; perhaps I won't like the new Tony, but I hope he will be back to normal with no more drinking binges and disappearing for days on end.

Last week the police came here looking for him because of the court case over the credit card fraud, and he told me he was going to run away. I rang Wendy, who said that I must persuade him to come home. She said he cannot run forever, he has to get it sorted. So he came home to sort things out.

When he gets picked up drink-driving they just lock him up and then let him out the next morning. He has lost his licence three times, but it does not worry him, he still drives. He just has no respect for anybody in authority, he hates it. I don't know how he gets away with it in court, because he talks to the judge like a piece of dirt.

My friends ring me up and say: 'Just tell him to go. Throw him out.' When they catch me on a bad day, when he has been out the night before, and I tell them that he did this or that, they say: 'You don't need him. Just tell him to go.'

Before I read that article I thought, I just can't take much more of this. I don't need this any more, and the children don't need it. But he can be so nice for a week or two that I think, oh, perhaps he has changed. Just as I get settled into that routine, he will go off the rails again. That is what it is like all the time. I might go and collect the kids from school, then when I get back he will say that he is going out and will be back at 6 p.m. But that doesn't mean anything. If he meets someone who asks him to go down to the pub he can't just have one or two and say: 'Right, I'm off home now.' Instead he says: 'Oh, just another one.'

With my asthma, I am ill quite a lot. The last time I was rushed into hospital he was out drinking. I had rung everywhere looking for him, but could not find him. I phoned a good friend who went round the pubs and found him. At 8.20 Tony rang me and asked what the matter was. I told him about the asthma attack and that there was an ambulance on the way. He said: 'All right, I'll get there before you.' I got to the hospital at nine o'clock. At two o'clock in the morning he walked in, drunk out of his brains. He had waited until everything was shut and then decided that he was coming over to the hospital. He doesn't understand how much that hurt: he thought that it was more important to stay out drinking than to come and see me. He knows that people can die from asthma attacks. I was lying there on a drip and the sister came in and said: 'Do you want to see your husband?'

I said: 'I don't want to see him. I want to kill him.'

Anyway, I told her to send him in and as he walked in I punched him, even with the drip stuck into my hand.

He does a lot of little things that hurt, things that my father would never do. Perhaps I compare him too much with my father, I don't know. On Mothers' Day he doesn't send cards, my mother does. That hurts. On our wedding anniversary he would not dream of buying me a card. Valentine's Day, Christmas, birthdays, I get nothing. I tell him that women like things like that, but he says he doesn't. He might not but I do.

When we were engaged I used to get roses, chocolates, cards and presents. Now there is nothing. He has changed in that way, too. Sometimes, when I am down, I would just like him to come and give me a cuddle, but he won't. I find that hard as well. He thinks he is too macho for all that. He doesn't think men do that, but they do. I know men who do that. My mother and father have been married 30 years and my Dad will still come home with flowers. I haven't had flowers from him for God knows how long, but he just doesn't understand that either. He never talks to me: we never sit down and have a conversation. He is either reading the paper or watching television. He will say: 'I'll talk to you later.' It is at times like that that I think I have had enough. I want to be able to sit down with someone and be able to talk to them. I want to know that when my birthday comes I don't have to depend on mother to do it all.

The other day, when it was his birthday, I went out of my way to make sure he had cards and I blew up balloons and hung banners in the house because he was forty. The kids had made him a birthday cake and he had promised that he would be in the house by five. He walked in at 9 p.m. and said: 'Oh, you've done all this have you?' The children's faces just said it all. I thought, I hate you. We don't need this.

I hope the therapy will solve all this, but until it happens I cannot say.

Unless you knew Tony very well you wouldn't come to our house. Some people have walked out because he can be just horrible. He couldn't care less if anyone likes him or not. I don't bring anybody to the house any more because of that. My mother and father get on great with him, and my mother will give as good as she gets. But if you came to our house as a stranger you would hate him, you would think, oh God, I wouldn't go back there again.

Someone came round to measure the windows some time back and he kept calling me babe. That night when he came back with the quote Tony said: 'Don't call my wife babe.' And he knocked him over the garden wall. So he never came back to the house again.

I don't have any counselling or therapy, just Tony. I

don't need any – I am normal. I hope that the nightmares and the drinking will go away and he will be normal.

Neither of us is working, so there is not much money about and we are arguing over things at the moment. Usually we do not have that sort of argument, so there is extra tension.

I just want to get it all over and done with and get back to normal. Then Tony can get back to work. I have been told that I will never work again because of my asthma. But I hope everything else will get back to normal and we will have regular money coming in. I want to take the children away on holiday, but I can't because we can't afford to. It is hard, because the kids come home from school and all the other kids are going away. I say that they know we cannot afford it. They say: 'If Daddy gave up drinking, we could.'

The only way I can get back at him for the way he behaves when he is drunk is to wait until he sobers up and tell him that the kids and I are leaving. I know he doesn't want that, and I know it will hurt him. He hurts me when he is drunk so I hurt him when he is sober. I think that it is as much my fault as his because I have a go at him when he is sober. I have my say the morning after, when he has a thumping headache and feels sick. I call him all the names under the sun, everything that I know he doesn't want to hear. At least I remember most of what I say to him, but he doesn't remember any of the things he says to me. I can see him being hurt as much as he has hurt me the night before.

I think if he had not joined the army none of this would have happened. I cannot wait until he has the treatment so we can get back to normal again.

Part 2

Women Who Fell in Love with Killers

In this section are the women who knew what they were taking on – or at least thought they did. Four of them met and married a killer; the fifth, Jane, wrote to a man on Death Row who became as close to her as family, so much so that she flew to Louisiana to plead for his life.

Jane joined Life Lines, a group which writes to prisoners on Death Row in the United States. Most of these men are poor, and many are black. Anybody joining Life Lines must accept that their prisoner has probably committed a terrible crime, rather than merely being the victim of a miscarriage of justice. Andrew, the man Jane wrote to, was found guilty of kidnapping the daughter of his ex-girlfriend and then raping and murdering her. He said he was drunk that night and had no idea whether he was innocent or guilty. He claims his defence lawyer was barely qualified and had not read the notes properly.

At the time of Andrew's trial he was portrayed in the local press as a monster. Jane believes that whatever he may have done he was no longer that person but had changed in prison. She made this plea to his Pardon Board hearing two days before his scheduled execution, when she was literally pleading for his life. She failed.

Mary's husband, Barry, put his hand over his aunt's mouth during a row to quieten her so that the neighbours wouldn't think he was hitting her. Whether she died of a heart attack or asphyxiation is still unknown. Barry, a working-class twenty-year-old overcome by guilt and re-morse, was advised to plead guilty. At the trial his solicitor did not turn up; instead he sent a junior who did not know the case. Barry was given the mandatory sentence for mur-der – life.

Lizzie, Mary and Tina, who are still married to their men, would all share Jane's view that whatever those men might have done in their youth they are now changed people. While the women find extenuating circumstances for the murders, they are equally sure that the men are so different now that they could not be repeated. Shirl Mahy from Aftermath emphasises that their trust is vital for such a marriage to succeed.

Queenie's marriage exploded in abuse and acrimony when her man was still in prison, she realised that he had not changed and that had they been living on the outside her life would have been in danger.

Except for Queenie, all the women who married killers found that the actual crime was the least of their problems. They put it firmly in the past. Rather, it is the conse-quences that they have to live with. Carrying on a relation-ship in prison, hidebound by rules and regulations, was the strain. For Mary and Tina, whose men have been released, there is the difficulty of resuming life on the outside.

Queenie

Queenie was interviewed anonymously because she still works in prisons and is worried that telling her story would mean that she could no longer work effectively. We met when I rang her to ask if she could put me in touch with any women to interview for this book. She decided that telling me her own story might help her to sort out her feelings. She married Dan, her fifth husband (who was serving a life sentence for murdering a woman), in prison, but the marriage did not work and she has since divorced him. In her late fifties she cuts a deliberately outrageous figure. She is still extremely hurt by the break-up of her last marriage and feels vulnerable. She wonders if now that she is sixty she will spend the rest of her life alone; a part of her dreads that and another part feels she could never share her house again. Her friends feel there will probably be a sixth husband. She is on good terms with her other ex-husbands, apart from Dan, and has four children. She was a successful businesswoman before deciding to join the voluntary sector to concentrate her energy on work around prisons.

I had been on my own for seven years and had been successful in forming a national voluntary organisation. This involved going to prisons from time to time, and during one of these visits I met Dan.

I had been invited to address a group of lifers about my work. He was there and offered to help with fund-raising, so I visited him a few times afterwards. We wrote to one another and we fell in love in exactly the same way as we would have done if we had met in any other place. I did not go for him because he was a killer. I am so used to killers, because I work with them, that the fact that he was a killer was of no particular threat to me; it would have been different for a woman from the outside.

He was very intelligent, which is always a prerequisite of mine in a man. He looked rather like an Old Testament prophet: he had a beard, a peaceful-looking face and steady eyes. He was also very open and honest in talking about his offence.

He had killed a woman when he was very drunk. He killed her in bed but he did not know who she was. He said he killed her because he was so drunk that he didn't know what he was doing, and so was she. He had thought, wrongly, that she was coming to attack him. He stabbed her because he had a knife and because he was paranoid and thought people were coming to get him. I didn't worry that it might happen to me when he got out. I think that is quite common with women: they always think it will not happen to them. I think, upon reflection now, that the amount of rage he had would probably have made him very threatening to me.

He talked easily about his crime because he is articulate, and because after six years of prison he was quite used to having to talk about it. The fact that he was telling it to me made it more difficult for him. He very deeply regretted it, but when it is more than six years away, it is hard to let people see how strong your remorse is. That is why I say that remorse is a condition of the heart. The Home Office talks a lot of rubbish about killers when they say 'he showed no remorse'. How do they know? It does not show on your face. It sometimes does not show in the words people say. That was why I felt that taking part in his remorse was very important. I hoped I was helping him to come to terms with it while he also tried to help me to come to terms with it. It was very hard work.

In my work I am used to talking to offenders about what they have done, who they have killed and why and how it happened. So it was comparatively easy for me to launch into the subject. The effect of this on him, compared with the other people that I was used to dealing with, was absolutely devastating. I was not at ease about it at all. I took on the guilt of his offence. I felt that by being in love with him, that was a natural progression. I had very great difficulty in coping with it. I anguished a great deal about it. The way I looked at it, and still do, is that if a woman is in love with a man who has committed a serious offence – and the more serious the offence, the more important it is – she has to be able to face it and deal with it.

Dan had already been in prison for six years when I met him, which meant he had committed his crime a long time before we fell in love. During the eighteen months before we were married, we thrashed through a great deal in our relationship. We examined one another's lives and argued about it. We wrote to each other every day, great screeds of intellectualising on just about every subject on earth.

In the end I came to the conclusion that the only way that I could tolerate the enormity of his offence was to help him to put his remorse into living practice. I had to find a practical way to even begin to make amends or show remorse of any sort. Tears and words were no use. I feel that remorse is a condition of the heart, so that condition has to be played out in real life. I had a determination to discover why it had happened and to deal with the build-up of rage and fury that had led to this appalling, tragic and totally wasted life. There had been no need for this death, no need for anything but his own rage. The girl had been completely innocent and had done nothing to deserve it. I felt that joining with him in the careful scrutiny of this build-up of fury within him was the only way that I could tolerate what he had done. I was in some way working to make sure that this appalling savagery should never take place again.

I regarded myself as a damaged person and therefore I felt I could understand him as a damaged person. His offence was not attractive to me, but I was more than prepared to take that on board. I felt that I had found in him someone who had a great perception of me and, of course, I was proved to be very, very badly wrong.

I had never met anyone who had paid so much attention to understanding me. Of course he had time to do that, while in the outside world you do not have time to do it, or you do not make time when you should. Maybe he had that perception and understanding and did not do the right things with it. I don't know. So I will never really know whether I was wrong or right, but, either way, I have used what happened to the benefit of other people.

I was interested in the effect of long-term imprisonment on people and I knew a good deal about it. It was neither an area that excited me nor a novelty to me, nor anything like that. When I was with Dan, some people used to say that it seemed to be terribly romantic: meeting a man and seeing only the best side of him across a prison visiting room. Don't you believe it. There is nothing romantic about a visiting room whatsoever. It is humiliating and degrading. Any show of affection makes you feel cheap and tawdry. My relationship with Dan, the whole way through, was one of careful control of our feelings. He felt very strongly that I should not be made a marked woman by too strong overt demonstrations of passion or affection.

I had a position of my own to keep up, anyway. In a prison visiting room, you see many tawdry scenes. I have it on the finest authority that people have actually had sex in visiting rooms. I find this utterly incredible and appalling, that a sexual thing should ever be used in such a way. I know it is easy to be judgmental, but Daniel and I felt very strongly about this.

Visiting rooms are places where you see the one you love and can therefore be places of great love and joy in many senses, but they are places where you feel shame and degradation at the same time. It is an amazing thing to see women who love their men walking up to the prison and then seeing them walking away. It is a terrible thing leaving your man inside, absolutely terrible. Anybody who thinks it is romantic just does not know anything about the situation. You have to wait and queue and are eventually allowed into the visiting room. In that particular prison the visiting room was dreadful, very, very poor quality indeed. It was like an M1 navvies' canteen: formica-topped tables, horrible tubular, uncomfortable chairs and the screws looking at you all the time. No carpet on the floor. There was an aperture in the wall where people could go and buy drinks and coffees, passed through by the busy beavers who are normally Women's Voluntary Service people, but in this case they were prisoners, who made the most foul-tasting coffee. Only the visitors, not the prisoners, were allowed to go to this little canteen hatch. No cigarettes were allowed. In those days I was a smoker, and so was Dan, and it was hard, nail-biting stuff to go without a cigarette as well as to go through all this trauma and emotion.

My husband would come into the visiting room, striding towards me full of love and joy, and we would just hug one another, almost wordless, with happiness at seeing one another. Then we would sit down and talk and hold hands, or touch feet under the table, or entwine our legs round one another's under the table, just to get closer, to touch the maximum area of each other's bodies. I used to smooth his arm or stroke his face which was really the extent of our love-making. I would give him the occasional kiss during the visit, but nothing more. I regarded, and so did he, anything more as wasting one's private life in public.

The humiliation of the visitors' room is that you are watched, even though you are a free person, on the right side of the law. It is an intolerable thing to love somebody who is on the wrong side of the law, because your whole world is turned upside down. You are a free person and you are with somebody who is not, and it is not quite as simple as you thought it might be because you are overshadowed by his guilt and his crime. The prison authorities are getting better at not despising the visitors like they used to a few years ago, but still you do feel that to a large extent they think of you as no more law-abiding than the person you are visiting. You feel humiliation because people are watching your every move.

With a convicted long-term prisoner like my husband, in those days visiting was allowed once a fortnight. It is getting a little bit more often now – you might be able to visit three times a month. But as Dan was 200 miles away, it was not easy. Even if you are in financial difficulties, the Home Office only helps you to get to the prison once a month. It was really very hard.

We are both very morally structured people. Both of us agreed that it did not seem right to be that much in love without getting married. I was surprised that he brought up the subject of marriage as early as he did, which was almost as soon as we realised we had fallen in love, and forced me to consider it. For both of us it seemed part of being in love. Personally, I wanted to marry him to show the prison authorities that I was taking the whole matter seriously. I wanted it to validate my position. I was also accused at the time of doing it to help my work, which it did rather, but that was not why I did it.

I had known Dan for eighteen months before the marriage. Obviously, it was not the sort of relationship where you went out to dinner, dancing or to the pub. That eighteen months would have been played out in the outside world in a far more careful and enjoyable manner. Instead it was intense and concentrated, exploratory and serious. So our progress in that eighteen months would have taken five or even ten years on the outside. Although it does not sound very long, it really was, and it represented a much longer development time than if we had lived normal lives.

Of course we had never lived together, which is a way of finding the cracks anyway, but our cracks emerged on different ground and for different reasons. I think that in the end we had different sorts of pressures. Although we did not live together, there were far more pressures on us than if we had.

The wedding was in prison and it was a wonderful day. It was a weekday morning. It was a beautiful chapel, and the governor and lots of his staff were there. We were allowed more guests and privileges than most people marrying in prison, because of the sort of prison it was. We were kept waiting twenty minutes at the gate. I think that was just because the prison officers were being particularly difficult. Two of my children came to the wedding. My third son was abroad and could not come, and my eldest son would not come. That was not bad batting really: three out of four on my side. My son and daughter who came were particularly loving and supportive and I was very happy indeed. I rejoiced in the commitment I had made.

Then we came into the chapel and my husband was waiting. There was a lot of rejoicing and people were very congratulatory and kind and supportive. It was wonderful and people believed that the marriage would work, because they had confidence in me. They thought, well, she would not dream of going into it if it was not something that she had seriously considered. Everybody knew that my husband was a serious-minded man.

It was really incredible. In the middle of our wedding vows on that summer day in the prison chapel, there was the most terrible thunderstorm. It was really quite dramatic, an omen perhaps. As we made our vows, the thunder was crashing. I smiled to myself at the time and thought, What a display of drama this whole thing is.

We were allowed to be together with our guests during the wedding reception after the ceremony, about two hours in all. However, we were allowed no time at all together alone, not a single second. We were allowed an extra visiting period. That was just dreadful, dreadful. Six of the wedding guests were allowed in as well.

The wedding was a very happy day, but the feeling when it is over, for a woman who has to leave her man inside, is unbelievable devastation. You know it is going to happen, you know you are going to feel it, and you are prepared for it, but it does not take away the devastation.

I am sixteen years older than Dan and this mattered not one jot in practical terms between us. A lot of prisoners fall

71

in love with older women, which is very interesting. I think it is partly because most women going into prisons are older. Young women are not usually interested in prison visiting or prison work, although there are a few. To go deeper into the psychology, the men who have killed young women feel they should reject them out of hand for the rest of their lives and do not feel safe with them. Perhaps they doubt themselves. There are a great many prisoners who fall in love with older women. So I was not in any sense surprised by this.

We used to have arguments about it, but we soon overcame them. I used to ask him what would happen when he got out and saw all the dolly birds. My husband used to wax very indignant about this, and said if he had found a woman twenty years younger than himself everybody would be slapping him on the back but because it was the other way round nobody thought that it was good. He thought this was both unfair and illogical. I agreed. So after the first few months the age factor did not come into it at all.

What destroyed the marriage was what destroys a great many. We were both very well aware of the pitfalls: we were aware that prison was a synthetic environment; I was very deeply aware that the things which trigger off violence are usually not present in prison. The things which made my husband do what he did were not there, or he might have done it again, perhaps. This is why it is always very difficult to assess somebody's risk factor when he comes out of prison. I was looking at this with as much objectivity as I could muster and I felt that we had to look beneath the surface of our relationship. We had to see if we could assess the pitfalls and we talked loud and long about it.

We wrote every day. It is very hard writing to somebody every day. One of my friends has written to her man every day for ten years, but now they can telephone each other every day. It requires a level of commitment that is unknown in another setting. The one thing that I felt very sorrowful about was the fact that my husband never really, fully appreciated my commitment. He never really appreciated what it had cost me emotionally to give him that commitment. He took it for granted and I think that was probably something that was basic in the breakdown.

I do not think he really valued me enough. He had not developed a grown-up grasp of it. He was too much the child within. He had reached the formula of it, but it took some time to realise that he had not got the whole concept deep inside him. I think I did the Home Office a favour, in the sense that I think it takes the intensity of a personal relationship to find the cracks in a man. He was, and had been, posing as a model prisoner for a very long time. I think the whole marriage break-up showed the rage that was still within him, and that that must have helped him to recognise it and work it through. So I think from his point of view, the marriage was very valuable. I have not allowed it to be wasted for me, but I wish I could have acquired that resource in another way that was less painful to me.

The irony was that the end came very suddenly in an area that I had hitherto never guessed would cause trouble. We were both very insecure and very jealous. Prisoners are known to be incredibly jealous, which is most understandable. I was in a job that entailed a great deal of travelling, and a great deal of meeting other men and other prisoners. I expected that this would trouble my husband and I offered him a great deal of loving reassurance about it. We talked about it at great length. But when the end came, it came very suddenly and his whole personality collapsed.

Out of the blue he accused me of having an affair with an officer in his prison. The arguments and the recriminations went on for a week or two, but it was very quick. I was absolutely shattered. I was deeply in love, totally committed and extremely besotted with him and it was just so appalling for me. The fact that he accused me of sleeping with a member of staff made it even more dreadful, because the other man was deeply mortified and embarrassed. He was put in a dreadful position, which fortunately was soon put right. Of course my husband had deliberately set out to do this, which made it even more painful.

I had not done what he had accused me of, although Dan made complaints against both me and the officer. The prison authorities were very fair about it and it was soon cleared up. What took much longer to clear up was the state of my emotions. In his autobiography, the author Laurie Lee talks about 'the untied parcels of my years', and this is my big untied parcel. I still feel it is a very untied parcel. A tragedy.

Things developed in such a way that I felt I had to get out. I did try to repair it, but I know enough about prisoners and the way that they think to recognise a breakdown when I see one. I got out rather than making it linger and cause unhappiness for everybody. It was completely mutual. It was not that I got out when he did not want me to.

We made one attempt to have a face-to-face argument about it in the prison visiting room, but it finished up in utter acrimony. He roared and ranted at me, saying that he never wanted to set eyes on me again. There was a lot of shame and degradation there and then. I gave up trying to get through to him that I was innocent of the charges against me. To this day I have seen him only once since and never spoken to him.

We had been married five months. It was almost as if, when he had got what he had set out to get, he could not handle it. My experience was far greater than his and so, in that sense, it must have been easier for me. I had a wider world in which I could recover, but, in many senses, my work was preventing me from being able to grieve when other people were looking at me. My responsibilities and the burdens of work were very great.

Looking back on it now, I had hoped that it would be a successful marriage. I looked on it as a plus that he was in prison. It might sound odd, but I was in my late middle age and I had had other relationships that had been distressing to me. I had been on my own for seven years so I was choosing not to get into another relationship that would have overwhelmed me and taken me over too quickly. The fact that we could not be together was in a sense the biggest plus we had, because we could take our relationship slowly and give ourselves the space we needed; and we were doing very well when he collapsed.

I think that it is particularly tragic because I was totally prepared to be celibate for the ten years he had ahead of him in prison. I felt that ten years was a very long wait. It was a terrible thing for me, but I did love the man very much and I was prepared to do that.

We talked about the age I would be when he came out and he found that he was quite comfortable with that. I think he felt that it would be a situation where he could be in command and take care of me. That appealed to him. Also, I would have been no threat at that age, which suited him well. It suited me, too, because I would have enjoyed somebody caring for me in my later years. We talked about this and both felt very comfortable with it.

That in itself was not the problem. The problem was that when he came up against the intensity of his feelings, his adult personality was not strong enough. He, like the majority of offenders, had been severely sexually abused as a child. This had stunted his development. It was the case of the child within him. Although he had learned the formula for adult behaviour, he had not learned to really live it out. This applies to a lot of offenders, but I had thought it did not apply to him. This is the irony of the whole relationship. I was aware of the major pitfalls, I knew it could happen but didn't think it would happen to us. It was really very sad, and it is still sad to me.

There is absolutely no possibility of me ever marrying another prisoner who is inside, because I have experienced the difficulties and the pain and I would not experience them again. If I got into a situation where I was emotionally involved with another prisoner, then I just would not marry him. I am not normally dogmatic about things in life but I wouldn't do it again.

I was utterly devastated when it finished, but I am a trooper and just keep going. I did not show it and very few people knew what utter devastation I was experiencing. When people are looking to you for help and support, they do not notice you. They only notice what they are getting from you. So I was able to disguise it quite well, but when you are disguising it all the time, it takes much longer.

I was not expecting him to change as I do not think that people do. I was expecting him to have formulated the reasons why he did what he did and I thought that he had. But he still had more rage in him than I reckoned with. It was not until this balloon was pricked that the rage came out.

I didn't marry him because I thought he would change; I didn't marry him because I didn't see him clearly. I married him because I loved him very deeply, because I was prepared to wait in order that during the remaining time he had to serve, ten years, I thought he and I would have made it. If he had been coming out the next year, I would not have married him. I felt that marriage was necessary to have that high level of commitment for the time that we had to wait. It was a long haul and I felt that he could have worked through his crime and our marriage within those ten years. By the time he came out we would have had a level of understanding to make it possible to live with. I was not in any way starry-eyed. I assessed what was possible and indeed it would have been if this hiccup had not taken place. I am sure of it, but the matter is over now.

One of the serious things against us was that his prison was the sort where they had therapy groups, which meant that everything that happened to us was taken and discussed in his group. We were living a marriage in public and that is absolutely intolerable, really dreadful. It might have been helping him but it was certainly doing nothing for me. Whatever went wrong he used to take to his group, or discuss it with another member of staff. I would be hopping up and down with rage, saying to myself: How dare he discuss what is going on in our marriage with somebody else? Of course, he was practically forced into doing that by virtue of the structure of the prison. It was very, very difficult. It has broken down more marriages than mine.

The break-up had a great deal to do with him being in prison. If this sort of crap had taken place outside, we could have had a screeching set-to and thrown things and roared. You cannot even show anger in a prison; you cannot do anything. You have to write it in a letter. In those days, the phone was a treat, not the right of a prisoner as it is today, with a phonecard. It would have been better perhaps if we had been allowed more phone calls, but we just did not have anything going for us at all. We had two hours twice a month and letters. I am not bleating about that part, because I knew before I began it.

I don't regret it at all. I learned a great deal. It is a long time ago now, and I never fail to be sad when I think of it. It has given me an enormous amount of resources to apply to other people and I have been able to help many a woman in the same position because of what happened to me. After all, it is not what happens to you, it is what you do with it. I feel infinite sadness and I still weep at my loss.

Lizzie

Lizzie is a nurse in the intensive care unit of a Surrey Hospital. She is married to Mark, who is in prison serving a life sentence for killing a woman. Lizzie is a committed Christian and became penpals with Mark after he converted to Christianity in prison. When she started visiting him their relationship gradually developed. Lizzie is exuberant and passionate about her job. I interviewed her in the maisonette which she has bought as the marital home for Mark and herself when he comes out. It is desperately in need of decorating, but she has decided to do nothing until Mark comes out so that they can make joint choices and the place can become theirs. When probation officers and prison officers started questioning her about whether she was a suitable partner for Mark, she says, she became fed up with being stereotyped. She stressed to me that just because she is a Christian it does not mean that she doesn't drink or that she has a dull life. Lizzie has multiple sclerosis, which at the moment has little effect on her life. She was furious when prison staff implied that having MS made it impossible for her to have a boyfriend on the outside and that she had started her relationship with Mark out of despair. At the moment their relationship consists of a two-hour visit twice a month.

My parents were divorced when I was young and, as there was very little money, I left school at sixteen, earlier than I had intended. I went out to work to help pay for the house where I lived with my mum. That meant I became a student nurse older than usual, at 25, and I went to Canterbury in Kent for my training, where I lived in student nurses' accommodation. I am a committed Christian and a girl who went to the same church as I did showed me a letter in a magazine from a lad in prison who had become a Christian and wanted someone outside prison to talk to. I wrote to see what would happen. I have always been a great one for penfriends and I write to people all over the world. The letter was in a national magazine and, as there were loads of replies, he gave a dozen letters, including mine, to a friend, who had also become a Christian in prison, and asked him to answer them.

The friend's name was Mark, and after I wrote back to him we continued corresponding. After nine months it seemed obvious that I should go and see Mark to put a face to the person I was writing to. I didn't think it was weird writing to him. He was just like all the other penfriends I have. I had a boyfriend at the time so there was no question of a relationship, but I did want to meet him.

Mark was in Long Lartin Prison in Evesham in Worcestershire. It took me six and a half hours to get there because I got lost and drove round for hours trying to find it. I was so late that I managed to get only the last fifteen minutes of the visit. Of course, he had not been able to give me any directions to the prison because he had been taken there in a closed van. He was very good about how late I was and he had thought I was not coming, which meant he was pleased I turned up at all.

When I met Mark, I did not fall in love with him or anything. He was just what I had expected. We had written an awful lot of letters to each other, and in one way we knew each other very well. Because there was no relationship, there was nothing to prove and it was terribly relaxed. I did not have to worry that I could not tell him something because he might change his opinion about me. None of that mattered. By letter we had already mentioned all sorts of things and I had told him all about training and my family.

Mark had told me that he was a lifer: I knew one does

not get life for pinching sweeties from Woolworth's and I realised that he could have committed any one of a number of crimes. However, at that first meeting, I asked him what he was in there for and he told me he was in for murder. He was very, very drunk while he was abroad and after various events, and being in the wrong place at the wrong time, he killed a girl. He has since explained how it all happened.

We carried on writing and I visited Mark every two or three months, partly because he did not get many visits and had very little contact with his family. At that time I considered him a friend and it seemed quite a normal thing to do, even if it was not a normal setting. He was supportive of me through my final exams, which was a stressful time as I failed my first lot of hospital finals.

Just after I qualified, things started going physically wrong with me and the hospital put me through various tests. They found that I had multiple sclerosis. It was wonderful having someone at the end of a letter I could unload on to, who was totally removed from the situation. It was what I needed. It was not so much that I was depressed, but I was nursing a lady with MS who died three days after I was told what I had, and it was a very difficult time to go through. A lot of the people I was living with were too close to the situation, but Mark was not involved. I felt I had nothing to prove – he was just there for me, and I could tell him anything. The letters between us carried on going to and fro and we discussed all sorts of things. The chap I was going out with at the time really could not handle the fact that I had MS, which did not help matters from my point of view. He kept telling me about the huge decisions he had to make in view of what I had told him, while I was just stuck with dealing with it all. I found that extremely difficult.

I went on visiting Mark every couple of months. Sometimes various friends would come up as well and see him. Quite often two, or even three of us would go up there. I took these different people up with me to talk to him so that it didn't get boring for him. It was quite ironic, really, because I was born in prison. My dad had been a civilian clerk in an open prison in the Midlands, and we had a staff house where I was born. Even so, I didn't know much about prison and the first time I went up to visit Long Lartin I was really struck by the starkness and harshness of it all. It seemed natural to go up and see him, just to cheer him up.

Eventually, the chap I had been going out with for two and a half years throughout this time, with all his big decisions, got too much for me, so I decided to go away with my mum. We went on holiday to Portugal. I talked myself out of the relationship. I needed to get away from it so that I could see how it was damaging me. When I came back, I swore that I was never going to have anything to do with men again.

Being pretty sure of what had happened, Mark chose my next visit to tell me how he felt about me. I cannot remember the words he used but he made it clear he was serious about me. He told me to go away and think about what I felt in return. He said it was really down to me, and in some ways he was taking a risk because I could have told him to get on his bike and that would have been it. As we are both Christians, it was a matter of thinking and praying about it. I was quite stunned to realise he had crept up on me when I wasn't looking. I really felt the same, but because there had been this other chap, there had been no question of a relationship and there had been no thought of it in my mind. My mum could see it coming because she had been up to visit about three months before, with me and another friend, and they had had a conversation after watching what was going on between Mark and I. They had been talking about what they could see, while I had been blissfully unaware of it.

I thought about the down side of it because, at the time, and even now, I do not know when he is going to be home. I certainly didn't know all of what was coming, like how you are viewed by the powers that be, the people in authority who began to have control over my life.

I knew what I would be taking on from Mark's point of view, because I knew him very well by then and he has always been very honest about his offence. I was not worried he would do it to me, but I might have been if he had not been so honest. The first time I asked him what he was in for, the answer came straight back and he was not guarded or vague. The prison authorities made sure that I knew absolutely everything about it; I think they were right to do that but the way they did it was not particularly good. I would not have put somebody in the position they put me in. Once his case officer and people like that were aware of what was happening, some things that he had written for them were given to me to read. He had written about all sorts of things, including the events leading up to his offence. Without excusing it, and I do not excuse it in any way, one could have seen it coming. My brother is not violent, but if you put him in that set of circumstances, you would have a violent result. Mark was nineteen and drunk when he did it. It does not cross my mind that he might turn on me because of the things that I know about it. We had already decided that when we had the time to sit and talk through all the minute details of his offence, we would. I already knew the generalities, but we needed real time to go over it in detail. If you are let in and out on time, it is a two-hour visit. That is not very long, and you are watching the clock all the time. We had decided that we would discuss anything that might crop up in the future and cause us problems and Mark's offence was obviously one of the things we had to discuss. We just felt that the best way for us to talk about the details would be in a slightly more relaxed setting, like his first home leave. However when we actually started talking about getting married we had to speak to the chaplain and the governor, and then he was told: 'You have got to tell her all about it now.' We had twenty minutes, after which Mark was locked up again and I had a 130-mile drive home. It would have been nicer to have a little more time to discuss it, because it was sort of 'Here it is,' and 'See you in two weeks' time.'

None of it was a great surprise, but being put in that position was far worse. Being married to a lifer was certainly not what I had intended. It was the last thing on my mind. In fact for a little while I tried to make sure that Mark did not get the wrong idea from the letters I was writing. When I started to write to him it was really on the basis that if he did get the wrong idea, he was going to be in prison for a while yet and the chances were that I would not be at the same address when he got out. If he did get the wrong idea I had decided I would just write and say: 'Look, this is not what I intended, let's call a halt to it.'

Although I had not planned on a wedding being the outcome, I still got wrongly stereotyped as the sort of woman who wants marriage without responsibility, or without sex, or who had some sort of hang-up.

My mum's reaction was quite bizarre. Out of all the blokes I have been out with, Mark is the only one she has totally approved of. I had been writing to him for about two and a half years when mum met him and it was love at first sight. They just sort of adopted each other straight away. She does not have much contact with my brother and Mark fitted in to the role of her surrogate son. He did not have any contact at all with his parents and he adopted my mum. They fell in love before we did.

All my friends knew that I was writing to him and my best friend had seen it coming for ages. They do not think I am mad, but I don't think they understand the situation; in fact several people have said that they cannot imagine what it is like. Unlike the authorities, they know me well enough to know that I did not dive into it on a romantic whim. The authorities have had moments when they have been totally irrational, mainly because they have seen it happen before. They presuppose all sorts of things about me and I feel they have judged me as the sort of person who marries a lifer rather than as me. They decided what I was like without getting to know me. What drives me mad most is that if they want to know something, they will ask me something completely different and draw conclusions from my answer about what they really want to know. I wish they would just ask straight out what they want to know. One particular chap concluded that I married Mark because I had MS and no one else would want me, which did not go down terribly well. They make references to class, saying that as I am middle class I cannot discuss my problems. In my view neither of those facts have any relation to each other, particularly as I have been called on to discuss some pretty private things with people I do not even know. Because Mark killed a female they discuss sex all the time, and that includes me: I have been called upon to discuss my attitude to sex, to previous boyfriends, who I have slept with and who I have not slept with and why I made the decision in each case. They want to know, or at least in theory their brief is to find out, if I am in great debt or if the area I live in is rough, but nobody has asked me these questions directly. It is like playing a game to which you do not know the rules and then being told that your move was wrong.

Mark told me how he felt in September 1989. After going away to think about it and realising I felt the same about him, I knew it was an all-or-nothing situation. I knew that I had to be serious and that what I was getting into had to end in marriage. It would not have been fair to tell him that I thought getting involved was a good idea and then a couple of months later change my mind. I gave it a lot of serious thought before I went back to him to say: 'This is how I feel, too.'

We got engaged in December 1989. In September 1990 Mark moved to a semi-open prison near Devizes, and we started talking about getting married. It was a matter of getting hold of the Home Office and asking their permission, and then it seemed as if we had to get permission from all and sundry. The prison chaplain, who was also a part-time vicar down the road, obviously knew that Mark and I were both Christians and wanted to get married in church. They would not let us get married in the prison itself, because they thought the guests would get hassled by the other inmates. We decided that we wanted to get married in the prison chaplain's church and we made a request to the Home Office and also to the Archbishop of Canterbury for a special licence. The chaplain gave us a date for the church but we had to plan the wedding without getting an answer from the Home Office. The Home Office gave permission for him to come out for the wedding less than six weeks before the big day.

The wedding, in April 1991, was absolutely wonderful. We were supposed to have 35 people but over 70 came. All sorts of people appeared. A couple of cars full of officers and staff from Long Lartin just turned up. A couple of officers and the prison governor were there and Mark's case officer was his best man. Mark had invited many of the people he had written to but never met, and they came. There were a few of my friends and my mum and stepdad. Apart from them and the people he knew from prison, Mark didn't know anyone at the wedding, but you would never have guessed that from the way he behaved. He was out for two hours and for that time everything seemed completely normal. An observer would never have guessed the real situation. We had a reception inside the church so that we didn't have to scoot off somewhere else and a lot of people from the congregation had cooked things and helped out generally. It was really nice.

When Mark's two hours were up, the taxi arrived and back he went, leaving me with no lift and only an hour to get back to the place I was staying at and change so that I could go and visit him, but I managed to do it. I had to hitch a lift back with one of the guests to where I was staying because the lady there had organised an old-fashioned sports car which I had gone to the church in, but we had forgotten about getting back.

People ask me how married life is. It is the same as being single, really. It is a bit strange. From Mark's point of view it was all over in a flash, because he was back in his prison uniform straight away. I have photographs of the wedding and somebody did a video for me, which I watch just to

86

remember the day, but he has not seen it yet. He wants to wait until he comes home and can watch it with me. The wedding has a dreamlike quality. I know it did happen but it really hasn't changed very much about us. He has had a couple of days out with case officers, when, officially, I was not there. He has been to our house, which I bought in the summer of 1992, for when he is finally released. He came out and was here for about six hours. The officers were very discreet and disappeared for an hour and a half, which was highly embarrassing because they knew what we were up to.

I miss him very much indeed, but I think I am luckier than women who have been married and their husbands have been whisked away from them. In those cases, quite often, things have gone on that they have not even known about; they are used to their husbands being there and all of a sudden they have disappeared. They are left to deal with everything, perhaps things they know nothing about. When my dad left my mum, she did not even know how to write out a cheque. She was left with all this stuff to get on with and didn't have a clue. She had to feel her way through it. It is a similar situation, but I am in control of what is happening out here, which sometimes has its down side. Sometimes I really want him home, because it is his home as well, and I am desperately trying not to turn it into mine. I have not decorated it and I do not intend to until he is there to share the decisions, because, if I do, it will be my house.

There are moments when it is really quite difficult. For instance, when I go to dos at work and everybody's husband or boyfriend is there while I am on my own. It is a bit tough at times like that. But at least I knew what I was getting into.

Mark has done thirteen and a half years so far, but the Home Office do not tell you when he is due out. Home leave has been mentioned as a possibility soon; we have a provisional date and I'm driving my work colleagues mad because I'm counting the hours.

I am not worried about the marriage falling apart when he gets home, because on visits you cannot do a vast amount apart from talk, despite what the media might say. We have got into a habit of talking, we do a heck of a lot of it and that is the way it has always been. Some people have problems with their marriages or relationships of whatever sort, but I don't think his offence will happen again and I don't have any worries about our relationship, because of the way it has gone. I know living together is very different to writing to each other, but that is the risk you take whether you marry someone or live with someone, or even share a house with your best mate when you go to college. You have to adjust to other people's habits.

The difficulty I did not expect was the attitude of people in authority. I did not like their preconceived ideas of what I must be like because I have put myself in this position. Nobody seems to find out if you have thought about it. There are people in the different prisons where Mark has been since we got involved who have gone to the trouble of finding out what our relationship is like, what sort of person I am, and how we interact. Some of them have said that they question people closely because they are a bit worried about women who get married to prisoners. One particular lady said that she had no worries about our relationship, because she thought it was very sound. However, when Mark and I first got together, I was absolutely terrified of her and she really put me through the mill. But she had satisfied herself that I knew what I was getting into. I know that they are trying to avoid people pulling out of a relationship because they cannot handle it and leaving the prison to deal with the emotions felt by the prisoner. Different people have treated me in different ways, and the prison he was in when we got married could not have been more supportive.

I feel very much on the outside because there are all sorts of discussions that go on about me in which I am not involved. They tell Mark that I feel one way or another about a subject without finding out whether I really do or not. I find that very difficult to cope with. In my job, I am used to treating people as individuals and realising that what I might see as a problem is not necessarily one for them. I have to find out from them if it is a problem before I say it is, or call it a problem on paper. My training seems to run counter to Home Office practice, where there are all sorts of suppositions about what I think or what I will do, and I don't like that.

I think that when he comes out, he is going to have a heck of a lot of adjusting to do. He has been in prison since he was very young. A lot of things have changed and there are going to be a lot of things to get used to. I don't think there has been much of an effort to rehabilitate him.

There is going to have to be a lot of work on the basic things. For instance, Mark has not handled even a small wage for all the time he has been in prison, and when he heard how much the mortgage repayments were going to be each month he was mortified. He was shocked when one of the officers told him about his wife's perm costing about £40. The next time he saw me, he asked rather worriedly: 'Is your hair naturally curly?'

He has no idea about all the things we take for granted. I think, in a lot of ways, I shall still have my work cut out for me when he comes home, because I will have to cope with a lot of the day-to-day things, like the household budgeting, until he gets used to it. He is not stupid by any stretch of the imagination, but he just has no experience of it.

I think Mark will work when he comes out. He is that sort of person. He is no slouch and he will do his utmost to get work. I don't think the prison service is terribly realistic about equipping people for work – if they can get it – especially the way things are at the moment. I will support him as necessary, but that is not unusual these days. We will sort out that kind of thing as and when we need to.

Tina

The problem for men who have come out of prison after being convicted of murder is that it is almost impossible for them to be treated normally by people they meet. They will always be a killer. Tina talked to me in the flat she shares with her husband, Billy. I wondered how Billy felt as he quietly listened to her talk and laugh about the problems he's had since leaving prison – being ten years out of date with prices and products, so he thought everything was far too expensive and had no idea how to use a video. Billy, a good-looking tattooed man in his thirties, sat with us throughout our interview and became slightly embarrassed as she described falling in love with him, but seemed quite happy to be just listening as she told her story. Her face lit up as she talked about him; she clearly finds him as wonderful now as when they first met. The consequences of unemployment, too little money and too much time have not harmed the relationship. Tina is in her late twenties and is writing a book about her life. Her office, where she toils away day after day, is literally a converted cupboard.

Tina and Billy live on the outskirts of a Midlands market town with a view of rolling hills from the window. Billy has served eleven years of a life sentence for murdering his fiancée's father when he was nineteen. He has a teenage daughter who lives in Manchester and visits him and Tina regularly. They are training to be counsellors so they can help people in prison and their families.

I was 24 years old when I met Billy. My life was a mess. I was working as a pub manageress and living with a man who was a lot younger than me, nineteen, and an alcoholic. It was an awful relationship and I still ask myself why I stayed in it.

A close friend of mine had been sent to prison for a petty offence. He was the one person in my life I could depend on. We had been through lots and lots together. Suddenly he was not there. I was probably at my lowest point at the time: I was in this terrible relationship, I had a chronically ill mother and everything else seemed to be going wrong. When my friend was taken away as well, it was like losing my lifeline. As I was a pub manageress, I was also being two people at the time. At work I had to keep up the appearance of this jolly, happy person while everything and everyone was just crumbling around me. I did not realise that what I saw as the final straw would turn out to be the best thing that happened to me.

My friend suggested that I write to Billy, who was with him in jail, because his family were not in regular contact with him. He wrote to me and said that Billy was a lifer and he wanted a penfriend. My friend said he thought someone should write to him because he was a really nice man. I thought it was typical of my friend to try match-making from jail, but I wrote to Billy saying who I was and what I was doing. He wrote back and from that very first letter he explained why he was in prison: he had got into a fight with the father of his fiancée, who had taken a weapon to Billy. Basically, Billy took the weapon off him, hit him and that was it. The man was dead. Billy was charged with murder. He and Billy used to have rows all the time, but Billy was devastated when he realised what he had done. He was only nineteen at the time. His engagement broke up after he went inside – not because of his crime, but because his fiancée was not prepared to wait.

At the time I read the letter telling me about it, I was so confused about my own life that it did not really register that he had killed someone. Anyway, it didn't really matter because I didn't think there would be any commitment. At most he was just going to be a friend, somebody I would probably visit occasionally, but mostly somebody to write to and someone to share my thoughts with. I certainly did not view a lifer as at all glamorous. He was just a penpal. It might seem strange, but Billy's crime has never been an issue.

We started writing to each other on 1 October, and on 8 December he was due to have a day out. He was at the stage of his sentence where he was allowed to have a day out every eight weeks and home leave every twelve. He wrote to me and asked if I would like to pick him up so that he could have this day out with me. I replied saying that I would be delighted to spend the day with him. By this time we had exchanged a number of letters, but I had never seen or visited him and I thought that I would love to meet him; it would be much better this way rather than across a prison table. I had to be checked out by a probation officer and everything was fine.

Billy was in Sudbury Prison and about two miles away there is a café called the Salt Box, which is where the minibus drops prisoners. I arranged to meet him there. I pulled up, Billy got into the car and within minutes of meeting him I loved him. I did not believe in love at first sight and thought it was nonsense. Yet I knew within minutes of meeting Billy that I wanted to marry him. That sounds so corny but it was true. I was still with this other man, but by that time we were just living in the same house and that was as far as it went.

Billy was just such a nice person. Then I felt even more confused: here I was sitting with this man who had killed someone. I will add that I have never ever felt in any danger, I have never been threatened by him. He would not threaten anybody. I knew I should not be experiencing all these feelings of love for him – I had only just met him and I didn't know him. It was such a confusing time. I didn't know the reason why I fell in love with him and I still don't know how it happened. Why does anyone fall in love? Nobody can know what someone is like just through letters, but I already knew him to a certain extent and I knew he was a caring person. And I knew I loved him.

We drove to my home. We walked around the park and went to see the friend who had introduced us and had just been released from prison. By the time we came back and cooked some lunch the day was gone and it was time for him to go, because I had to get him back to the prison by five o'clock. It had been wonderful. We had spent the day talking as if we were old friends who had known each other for years, like any conventional couple. I didn't want to take him back. As I was driving along the lonely country roads I just wanted to drive away with him and keep him, although it would have been totally stupid. When we arrived at the prison gates I got out of the car, intending to simply hug him, but the most natural thing in the world was to kiss. That may sound awfully cheap, but it wasn't, it was very natural. It was not planned by either of us, it just happened. By then I was completely confused. He just walked down the long drive to the prison and was just sort of gone, with the promise of a visiting order (which prisoners have to send to people to allow them to visit) in the next post.

Driving home I was completely muddled. I knew how I felt about Billy but not how he felt about me. At the time Billy had been very hurt, not just by the prison system, but by everything around him. He was building this wall around him to keep everybody out, and he was determined that nobody was going to get through it. I was sure that he did like me, but I just didn't know whether he felt anything more and I knew it was going to take a lot to get through to him. However, I thought he was worth working on. I also had the compulsion to get home quickly to write him a letter to let him know how I felt. I still have that letter – Billy kept all his letters from prison – and reading it now, it just seems so stupid. God knows what he must have thought when he received it. I sound like a demented woman, but I needed to tell him. I needed to be straight with him and give him the chance to say no, if that was what he wanted.

The visiting order arrived as promised. I could not wait

to go and see him. I ended my relationship with the other man. He moved out, back to his father's, and I was living in my little house all on my own. My decision to end the relationship was not just because of Billy, although that was a factor in it – I just felt it was time to move on. Even if Billy did not feel the same about me it was time to get my former relationship into proportion and put it behind me to ensure that there was space for a relationship between Billy and me if anything developed. I decided that if there was to be a relationship, it would be Billy's choice, and I made it clear to him I would still be there as a friend, however he felt. I knew he was a special person and needed someone on the outside. I would still go on visiting him and he could come to my home for days out whatever happened. I went to see him on the next visiting day and he made it fairly clear that he felt the same. I had already received a reply to my emotional letter saying that it was not silly and he understood how I felt. Looking back on his letter now, reading between the lines, I can see that he was trying to tell me that he liked me a lot. He made it quite clear that he did not love me, but at that time I don't think he was capable of loving anybody. He did not like to put much in his letters, because they were read by the prison officers. During the visit he made it clear that although there was not a relationship, there probably was going to be one. But that stage is really a blur in my memory, because there were so many emotions, total confusion. Everything was just a mess.

Billy managed to arrange visiting orders every week. As I worked mainly at night, I found that quite easy. I don't know how he managed it because visits were supposed to be fortnightly. The letters became daily as I just had to write to him, like any conventional couple coming home and talking about the day's events. It was like a diary, but I was talking to Billy. He wrote to me twice a week. The letters and visits carried on until February, when he was due for a home leave for the weekend. He decided that he wanted to spend his home leave with me. It meant that more probation officers came round to check me out. The whole situation was so new to me that I saw them as the enemy, which is how Billy had always put them over. In fact our probation officer is OK. She lets us get on with our life. I did not realise that I was being 'vetted', as the head probation officer in Rugby put it at the time. He was a wizened old man and could not understand the situation. I just answered all the questions so that I could get Billy home for the weekend. I just tried to conform and keep them happy. It worked, and he came home.

We went to the Cotswolds for half the weekend and up to Manchester for the other half. We had to get to know each other, but I wanted it to be away from my home. I thought we should be on neutral territory. By this stage it was fairly obvious that a serious relationship was developing. The weekend was absolutely wonderful, everything was just so natural, as if we had always been together, although we had known each other for only five months.

We had no secrets, which was important. Of course, Billy could not have secrets from me – being in prison he had to be straight about everything, because if he did not tell me I would find out from a probation officer or prison officer – but he never wanted to hide anything anyway. Because Billy was open with me, I felt I had to be open with him and we are still the same now, we have no secrets. In Manchester we saw his family. I was introduced to his sister as a friend, but thankfully she saw through it.

The drive back from Manchester on the M6 was just awful. After being with him for a few days I just did not want to let him go. However, going over the Manchester ship canal, he told me that he did not love me and he could never love me. At that stage I am sure he did not, but it wasn't what I wanted to hear. He was probably still incapable of love, but the wall was coming down slowly. I think the relationship developed from there. We had had a good weekend together – we knew each other better by then, and having spent a few days together, we realised that we could cope with each other. When I took him back,

I accepted that he had to go and it was just part of our relationship if I wanted it to go on. It was my choice, and having chosen I just had to put up with it.

We were hoping for his parole in August, which was something to work for. When Billy returned on the Monday, he was summoned to the board to be told that he had got his parole, which was much quicker than we expected. It was just a matter of waiting for a place in a pre-release hostel. Then he would have to do nine months there before being allowed to go home.

He wrote me a letter when he got back to prison from our weekend together. It was Billy's usually chatty letter and he just dropped in one little sentence saying that he had got his parole. I did not understand what he meant, I just could not register it. I took the letter to a friend, who could not understand why I was crying my eyes out. I was elated that he had got his parole, but I felt panic that he would not want to know me. He would go back up to Manchester, which was the plan at the time.

We just carried on with the letters and visits until he went to the hostel, which was on 25 March 1991. The hostel was in Nottingham, only an hour away from my home. He settled in fine and he was there about three weeks before he was allowed his first visit home, because they feel the men have to settle in. He found himself a job within a few days; he worked in a slaughterhouse, which was ironic. He hated it because he had been in prison for murder and got a job killing these poor pigs, which was just what he didn't want to do. But it was a job and it paid the rent at the hostel and allowed him to come home at weekends. He just started turning up at Rugby – there was never a plan that he would come here for his weekends home, it just happened, as it seemed the natural thing to do.

He started coming home every Friday night and going back on Sunday night. The relationship was really building up because we were now like a normal couple. There are so many people whose husbands work away during the week. He was accepted by my friends without question, but we did not have many. We have made our friends basically round our families, particularly mine, and around people we can trust. We are quite happy on our own anyway.

By this time Billy had almost committed himself to me, not directly, but in roundabout ways, and I knew he was getting serious. One day when I went to the hostel to pick him up, I found him in the car park and he said that he had been looking for me out of the window. I was a bit surprised because I always turned up at five o'clock. He said that his heart went flip when he saw me, and I thought to myself, this is it. I have done it. We got engaged the next weekend, in May. I had finally got through to him.

I had stopped working at the pub just after Billy started at the hostel and I was on the books of a temping agency because that allowed me to work when I wanted to work and still be there for Billy. While he was in prison, the pub job had not been a problem because most of the work was at night. Nobody in the pub knew what was going on: they would not even have begun to understand. I would just have been a scandal – it would have been a *News of the World* job.

I was so happy when we got engaged, because that was the commitment I wanted, and we started planning to get married. He was due to be released on 25 December that year, which was not a very sensible date, but the Home Office was very good and released him a few days early. He had kept coming home every weekend and we decided we should get married the day after he was released. Now we are just a happily married couple. All the way through our relationship it's like we have always been together and being married is a bonus. Billy is my best friend.

He had been in prison for eleven years and when he came out there were so many new inventions that it came as a shock to him. He was even surprised at the new-style phone boxes. Only last night he was introduced to instant custard just made with water, which he had never seen before. He could not believe Pot Noodles or any of the instant meals. The first time we went to Tesco, we got to the till and I was about to pay the bill, which was around £40, when Billy said: 'How much is that? It's disgraceful.' He could not believe the price of shopping. When we went to buy a pair of jeans he expected to pay £7.99 and we were looking at about £35.99. There was a dreadful scene in the shop when he started saying: 'I'm not paying that price.' Of course, he had no idea about videos. He still will not touch the one we have at home.

They were all amusing incidents but it was as if Billy was learning to live again. In some respects he was still nineteen, the age at which he had been sentenced. Everything had to be done in such a hurry. He would wait for nothing and everything had to be done now. He would not take no for an answer.

People have said to me that I was so lucky meeting Billy at the end of his sentence and we have discussed whether I would have stayed with him if he had been only halfway through or at the beginning of his stretch. I think I would have stayed; it was just a bonus that he was paroled so early. When I decided that I was committed to him I didn't know whether he felt the same and I had no idea how the prison system worked. I did not know what parole was. As far as I was concerned Billy was doing a life sentence and life meant life. I had quite a sheltered upbringing and Billy has opened my eyes and educated me.

It was difficult to accept, at first, that a lifer's sentence does not stop when they leave jail, because neither of us knew what to expect from the probation service. It is something that is always in our minds although we do not dwell on it. We call Billy's probation officer the other lady in his life because she is. If we want to go to see Billy's family we have to telephone her and explain that we want to go away and where we are going. We have found that if we play fair with her, she will be fair with us. We only go to see her once a month now, but at first it was once a week. She usually comes here and she is very nice – our age and chatty – and I think we are lucky in that respect. She lets us get on with our lives, and if there is a problem we know where she is.

Luckily, I never had much to do with the prison officers. However, when I went to see Billy they recognised me from visiting my friend and sometimes I felt that they thought, 'she's one of them'. It might just be me feeling paranoid, but I felt like a prison groupie. I could almost hear them saying: 'One minute she's seeing that one and now she's here again seeing this one.' I learned to just smile at them. Billy sheltered me a lot from the prison officers – several times he said they wanted to see me but he would try to get me out of it. He felt very strongly that he had committed the crime and there was no reason why I should pay for it, although if there was a problem, I would be behind Billy all the way, 200 per cent. Nothing would have barred me from seeing him, nothing at all.

The funny thing is that if Billy had just been a person on the street whom I had met when I did, I don't think we could have even been friends, because I was in another relationship and I couldn't have stood anyone around me. The way it worked was that I saw Billy when I wanted to see him. It sounds very selfish, but it meant I could take it at my own pace.

I don't really know whether he had an incredible reaction to finally being released because with our wedding the next day and then Christmas it was all mad, and we did get drunk for a week. Now, we like the quiet life. We just sit in in the evening and have a couple of cans of beer. We really enjoy each other's company, which is very lucky as I was made redundant last September and neither of us is working. When I first lost my job I panicked, wondering how we were going to survive. I didn't know how I was going to live with him all day because I had been used to working twelve and fourteen-hour shifts. Our marriage has grown stronger because we are together and we do everything together. We are both training to be counsellors for prisoners and their relatives at the moment. There are no jobs out there which I would like to do and am qualified for. I would rather be doing a job helping other people than a conventional job, and so would he. It would also be a job where I could talk about my husband – can you imagine doing that in a typing pool?

Recently I spoke to a lady who told me I was very brave to marry a lifer. I replied that I was not brave, simply in love.

Mary Rutter

Both Mary Rutter's sons have learning difficulties. She brought them up alone after she left their father when they were tiny. She met her second husband, Barry, when her children were teenagers and he was completing a life sentence for murdering his aunt at Ford Open Prison near Bognor Regis, where she lives. Barry has now been released and the family live together in a council house. None of the family is able to work. Mary asked me to go down to see her because she feels that the criminal justice system has let Barry down. She believes that he should never have been convicted of murder, only manslaughter, and that the prison system does not help prisoners return to the outside successfully.

I visited Mary and Barry on a cold day in March. We sat and shivered in the dining room as the gas fire flickered on little more than the pilot light and they kept themselves warm with cigarettes and tea. The British Rail timetable dictated that my visit was between midday and two, and as the hunger pangs started I realised how insensitive I had been, for they could not possibly have afforded to feed me. With all four of them unemployed and with no prospect of any of them getting work, they live in hopeless, grinding poverty.

While I was there the elder boy returned from London, where he had moved to try to lead an independent life and hoped to find more opportunities for work. There was no work, and the loneliness drove him home, back to a cramped house and strained relations with his stepfather. Mary is a large, strong woman, both physically and emotionally, but she enjoys being able to lean on a man after so long alone, even though it is still she who runs the house and makes the decisions. She certainly experiences problems living with a man who has served a life sentence, but feels that they are more than compensated for by the happiness that Barry has brought into her life.

My first marriage broke up when I realised my husband was an alcoholic. I had two boys and I wanted to give them as normal a childhood as possible, which they could not have with an alcoholic father, so I brought them up on my own with the support of my friends. My eldest son, Andrew, is aphasic, which means he cannot read or write, and my younger son, David, is mentally handicapped, so they both went to special schools.

When Andrew was sixteen, he said to me: 'It's time you thought about getting married again, because one day I'm going to be leaving home and David will go his own way and you'll be left on your own. I don't think that's a very good idea.'

I explained to him that marriage is not like getting a turkey out of Safeway – you cannot just go and get yourself married because you want it. It is something that happens if it happens. If it does not, well, you have lost nothing.

I moved to Bognor Regis in 1986 and again my son urged me to marry. At that time the children were involved in a programme called Reach Out at Ford Prison, which was about six miles away. The men had the care of the children under supervision and entertained them for the morning, playing indoor games. During the summer holidays the governor gave them permission to go outside the prison and take the children to Butlin's or Alton Towers for the day. Every day for a fortnight was taken up with this.

Andrew, being chatty, soon told one of the men, Andy, about my situation, which I was not too pleased about. Andy invited me to go down to the Brent Lodge Wildfowl Trust. He said he would like to help me as well as the children, because he had become very fond of my elder son. I made it quite clear to him that I was only going for the children's sake and I did not want him thinking there would be any romantic links between us. It is very common for people who have been locked away for that length of time to want to get involved with women as soon as possible. Like everything else, if you have been deprived of something that is the first thing you want. I had to spell it out to him right from the start that the only reason I was going was because of the children.

So I started going and I met Barry there. For the first two days I thought he was just another worker. I didn't realise that he was also out working in the sanctuary as part of his pre-release scheme. I fell in love with him, and luckily it was a two-way thing and it was quick.

One of the things which first attracted me to him was that nobody had ever paid much attention to David, my younger boy, because you have to say things twice to him before he is able to understand and give a meaningful response. People get very irritated with him and they don't have the patience to say everything twice, but Barry did. When I first saw Barry he was on his hands and knees scrubbing out the cage and David was chattering away, which he did not normally do. Usually he was quiet and stayed in a corner out of sight, and yet these two seemed to be getting on like a house on fire. It was great.

Another day when I went up there Andy said it was time to take the feeds out, which involved driving a very low-powered tractor with the buckets of food on two trailers on the back. It was quite heavy. David said: 'I can drive a tractor.'

'If you can drive a tractor, you can drive this tractor. Sit on the tractor,' said Barry. I was in a complete panic. I dreaded what David would do with a tractor in his hands, I didn't realise how slow it was. Barry stood there telling him what to do and watching him. He really had faith in him and that is so important.

Another time Barry was wheeling a wheelbarrow with a funny fluffy bobble hat on. He thought he looked really funny; I thought he looked gorgeous. That was when I started to fall in love with him.

I started going down there all the time. I was cleaning out cages, washing these oil-streaked guillemots – or at least he was washing them and I was drying them with a hair-dryer – and we would be larking about. I went for one day and ended up going every day as a volunteer. Then the man who ran the place asked if I would do his cleaning for him, so I got paid for doing that.

I was told that Barry was a prisoner after about two days. I didn't really think anything of it at the time. I certainly didn't know he was a lifer. When I found out that he was in prison it didn't shock me because I had got to know Andy, and because I had done prison visiting before. When I was bringing up my two children I thought that I would like to do some voluntary work, but I wanted to fill a gap, not just go and work in a hospital library or do fund-raising for sick children, because there were so many other people far better qualified than I was doing that sort of thing. I wanted the type of work that not many people would be interested in, so I decided to start prison visiting. I went on a course and qualified as a prison visitor. Then I joined the New Bridge [an organisation for prisoners], which was run by Lord Longford at the time, and I did that for four years. All the course tells you, basically, is how prisons are run, a bit about sentencing, a bit about what it is actually like in prison, what sort of backgrounds the inmates come from. I found it fascinating that you can get somebody with a degree, who is extremely well educated, in for fraud alongside a burglar who comes from a council estate. I found the contrasts between the two quite interesting.

They said that the last thing you should do is get involved emotionally. It is rather like nurses in hospitals not getting too involved with their patients. I carried out the work that I did on that principle. It was great; I thoroughly enjoyed it. So when I found out that Barry was a prisoner I had the feeling it was almost fated, because I had the education to know what I was doing, know what I was letting myself in for. I remember feeling how weird it was, after doing four years of prison visiting and not getting involved at all. I had the opportunities but I didn't, because it would have been wrong. To then end up with a prisoner was quite funny, really.

When Barry told me what he was in there for, I thought it was very brave and honest of him. Nothing would have been easier than to have told a lie or pulled the wool over my eyes. That showed me how human he was. He was in for killing his aunt. While I do not excuse it I can rationalise it, because being a twenty-year-old man he was pushed too far, and we have all been in situations where we have been pushed too far. Unfortunately he stepped over the line. They were having a row and she was shouting at him. He was worried that the neighbours would think he was beating her up, so he tried to shut her up by putting his hand over her mouth and she died.

One pathologist said that she died of a heart attack and another said that she died of asphyxiation, and nobody bothered to find out which one it was. I find that utterly incredible. The more you get into the legal system the more you realise that you are dealing with an absolute snowball effect. He should not have been charged with murder, because it was clearly manslaughter, and no way should he have done fifteen years in prison. It is absolutely horrendous. On the day of the hearing his own solicitor did not even have the courtesy to turn up. They sent his deputy, who read the files in ten minutes, went before the judge and said: 'Guilty.'

The judge turned round and said: 'Unfortunately, Mr Rutter, you have pleaded guilty. You leave me no other course of action.' He was really telling Barry that if he had pleaded not guilty he would have got about seven years for manslaughter. Barry says those words have always stayed in his mind and he has never forgotten them.

I do want to stress that it is neither Barry the murderer nor Barry the ex-con I am married to, because I did not initially meet him as that. I met him on a one-to-one basis as Barry the man; that is who I met and that is who I fell in love with. All the rest came later – admittedly only days later, but you can fall in love like walking into a supermarket and bumping into somebody. Whether you meet them in a disco, a pub or wherever, you do not know all about their past, you just know what you see. And if what you see is what you love then that is the way it is. I think he has been treated abominably by the rules, which does not give you any faith in justice at all. And I am utterly astounded that they did not even bother to get the correct analysis on the death certificate. There are no words to describe my anger and frustration.

For about eight months we saw each other every day at the bird sanctuary. We could not go out in the evening because he had to go back to prison – he was only let out for the day. He was collected from the train station in the morning and returned there in the evenings, so I saw him only in the hours that he was actually there. We did manage to be alone some of the time because it was a big place, and we ignored the birds squawking around us.

Barry was due to be released from Ford in January 1989. I met him in October 1988. He had to go up to London to live in a hostel and came home to me at weekends. He came here every weekend for six months. It was very nerveracking because we were on our best behaviour for the first few weekends and there was quite a lot of strain. As we got to know each other better we started to relax, but I found it very hard that he would have to go back on the Sunday night. I would look forward to it all week and it was over before I could turn around. It seemed like now you have him, now you don't. I couldn't settle down, it was too disruptive.

Barry and I have differing views on the hostel situation. I believe society would benefit greatly if the families that are going to have a long-serving prisoner returned to them on a permanent basis were given counselling. If the prison service did that, then when the prisoner was up for release he would have a hell of a lot better chance of settling down. There were all sorts of problems that I had never even thought about. If people like me were warned about this and the reasons for Barry's behaviour had been explained to me, I would have been able to understand it and then found ways of working round it, or at least compromising. It would save a lot of heated rows, quite honestly, that are at the end of the day over nothing.

I think the hostels are non-productive because they expect the former prisoners to go out and get themselves a job, and hold down that job for the whole six months, when they have been away from society and are slap in the middle of London, of all places. Barry's hostel was a house in the grounds of Wormwood Scrubs Prison, out in East Acton. They had to check in every night by eleven o'clock and they were out by eight in the morning. If they hadn't got a job then they went down to the job centre where a lady who was aware of the situation pulled all sorts of strings to get them in employment. But when they have been away from society and are put smack in the middle of London and given enough money for their fare to the job centre and back again, it is too much. It is too soon and too much. They should be counselled and it should be done gradually.

Barry had a job as a road-sweeper. Unfortunately, a few weeks before the end of the hostel period, he got himself into trouble, drinking and driving, and was promptly put back inside again. What do you expect when most of them finish work around seven or eight in the evening, and they know they do not have to be back until eleven? What are they expected to do? They can't see their families. All these men together, who have been locked up for God knows how long, what do they do? They go to the pub. What else is there to do? There is nothing organised for them. There is a telly, but they have been watching that for years so they are not going to be sitting down watching telly, are they, playing happy families? They are going to be up to mischief, aren't they? It sticks out a mile to me.

I found it difficult because it was so frustrating, knowing what would be happening, but being miles away from it. There was nothing I could do about it. I was helpless. You can see something is going to happen and you have to stand there and watch – I can't think of anything worse. It is like two cars coming down the road: you can see that they are going to smack into each other, but you can't warn either driver, so you just have to stand there and watch them smash and get messed up. It doesn't matter who you tell because it does not change anything. It is going to happen.

Barry was put back into prison and we did not know how long it was going to be. It turned out to be two years. He spent seven months in Wormwood Scrubs, a closed prison; then he was transferred to Leyhill Open Prison in Gloucester. I went every week to see him.

The second time he was in that London hostel I was really on tenterhooks. I was quite ill with it by the time it had finished. He was working on the buses, at Stamford Brook bus garage, as a cleaner. I thought, here we go again, back on the same treadmill. He kept saying to me: 'You haven't got to worry, I'm going to get through this hostel. I messed it up last time but I won't mess it up again.'

It was not that simple, when I was stuck here Monday to Friday, knowing all the temptations, what was going on and how easy it was to have one too many and do something silly. I found that extremely difficult. I decided that if I got him to phone me up it would give him something extra to think about. If I had felt that something was going wrong I think I would have gone up there and tried to sort it out. It sounds stupid, I know, completely irrational, and I knew he hated it. But I didn't exactly enjoy sitting around waiting myself.

I was so relieved when it was all over. I can't tell you how relieved I was. He finally got out and came to live here and he has been here ever since.

We had married while he was in Leyhill, on his last home leave. In those days they were allowed out for four days on a home leave every three months, the prison's idea of trying to get them closer to their families. However, no sooner are they home than they are going; it is the same as with the hostels. The last time we decided to get married. We did it because I am an all-or-nothing person; I either am committed to somebody 100 per cent or I am not. I do not play at life. I never have and I never will.

Barry asked me to marry him in the visiting room in Wormwood Scrubs. What a romantic place to ask someone to marry you! I couldn't imagine anywhere worse, really. He said to me: 'Will you be my wife?' I didn't answer him the first time. I thought, I am not hearing this properly. I was stunned. He repeated it and I thought, he's serious. He means it.

I said: 'Yes.' I do believe very much in commitment.

My dad was very good about it all. He was 72 and he had seen me through one wonky marriage, he had seen me on my own and there I was turning round to him in the kitchen and saying I was going to get married again, and to a lifer. He told me that I had to remember that at the end of the day Barry was in for murder, and it was a woman, and who was to say that if he ever really lost his temper I would not be next on the list. I told him it was a possibility, but no more of a possibility than if I lost my temper and ended up skewering him. That is the risk we are talking about. He said that if I knew him and I was sure that what I was doing was right then he would back me 100 per cent. I was very relieved to hear him say that. He did get to know Barry because we met him several times and went out with him, and I was very pleased about that. My dad died before the wedding but he was really pleased about us being together.

We had a quiet family wedding in Chichester with about 30 guests. My sons thought it was great. They were over the moon. The boys did not really realise what having a dad was all about because they had not had one for ten years. They were too young to remember anything particularly nice about having a dad, so it was a novelty. When he came home permanently to live with us it was all great as far as the boys were concerned. David was very excited; so was Andrew, but he was more cautious, because he had been the man of the house and he hadn't stopped to think that when Barry came home for good he would no longer be top dog. He found handing over extremely difficult. There were problems on both sides but we just worked through them.

There was no job, or prospect of a job, for either Andrew or Barry. That does cause tension and friction. Nobody wants to spend the rest of their married life living on income support. I can't think of anything worse. I didn't know what to do for the best, really. It is so annoying having skills and not being able to use them, but there is no real chance of employment. We have now been living together for three years, and on the whole it has been good. We have had our ups and downs.

When Barry came to live here, my friends had different reactions. Some of them I have never heard from since, but at the end of the day they were not really my friends. I don't worry about it. The true friends stood by me and continue to do so, and they are very supportive of David. One friend in particular, Sue, picks David up every Monday night, takes him to the youth club and brings him back – we don't have a car and it is a good two miles away, a bit too much at that time of night, doing the journey twice. She takes him to football every Saturday afternoon, she and her husband. Her husband plays and David loves to go. So I do have some very good friends.

Then there are the neighbours. Barry next door was very against the whole idea. He was very wary of my Barry. However, by and large Barry is accepted socially and that is a big step.

When he first moved in a section of our fence had blown down. Barry went down to the club and the two next-door neighbours were there and offered him a drink. One of them said: 'Any idea when you can fix the fence?'

Barry said: 'Give us a chance. I've only just come home. It's my first weekend home.'

'Where have you been?' asked the neighbour.

'In prison.'

'How long did you do?'

'Fifteen years.'

'Fifteen years! What the hell did you do?'

'Murder.'

'Well, forget the fucking fence.'

He was fine after that.

What has really helped me deal with all the problems is Aftermath, which was set up to help the relatives of offenders. It is a charity, the first one of its kind. It is really brilliant. I go to the meetings once a month and we give each other help and support, which is very much needed. Some people are still going through the trauma. Some people have got their husbands or wives coming home and don't really know what to expect, because it is not what you think. It is not like somebody just moving in. It is somebody who has been deprived of this, that and the next thing and all they want is to satisfy that craving for what they have not had. It can be extremely wearing.

Freedom is the first craving, and their perspective of freedom. Barry's perspective of freedom at that time was walking out of the front door whenever he felt like it and walking back through it again whenever he felt like it. Now, the way I was brought up, if you go through the front door you turn round to whoever is in the house and say that you are just going round the paper shop and will be back in ten minutes, or you are going for a long walk and will be back in two hours, or you are going up to Chichester and will be gone for the best part of the day. That is fine. I have no problem with that whatsoever, whether it is ten minutes to the paper shop and back or all day at Chichester – it doesn't worry me, but I do like to know. I don't like it when I hear the door close and I am thinking, where has he gone? Will he be back for dinner? What if I go out and do the shopping and he comes back and sees there is nobody there? Will he then get the huff and go off again?

It throws you into quite a quandary as to what to do for the best. When I said this he thought it was like being back in prison. He called it a ball and chain. He said: 'You will have me signing out next, and signing back in.' He got very defensive about it. Then when he saw the kids saying: 'I'm going up so and so's, I'll see you in a bit, Mum,' everything was OK.

He hated it if I asked too many questions. I was not suspicious, I was just being me. I do not think I am a particularly nosy person, but if I asked more than three questions in an hour, he would say that I would have him reporting for duty next. That was his attitude. It was like he was saying to me: 'Don't talk to me. Don't look at me. Don't question me. Don't do anything, just let me be.'

But I was not singling him out. I was the same with whoever was in the house, whether it was friends or family. He took his frustration out on me rather than trying to see how it is living in a family.

Then, of course, we had the eldest boy performing all over the place, because he was having to hand over; then we had David in the background throwing a wobbly over something else. So it is difficult. This is why I stress the need for counselling, so that you know where you are. You are walking into a minefield and unless someone has tagged those mines there is a good chance you are going to get hurt. I think something should be done about it.

The biggest problem is that Barry is not free, not in my book, anyway. He is on life licence, which means he is monitored for the rest of his natural life. Even when he dies the Home Office will send their pathologist to get his fingerprints. Not even in death do lifers have dignity.

For the first few months after coming out he had to report once a week to the probation officer, then, as time went on, once a fortnight and then once a month. He has to have this contact for five years. I think that is a hell of a long time. Like everything it does work both ways – the probation officer is brilliant, really brilliant, but he has too many lifers scattered over too wide an area, so he does not get a chance to do what he would like to do. It is very limiting and very frustrating for him, as it is for all probation officers.

Barry cannot spend the night away from this house without phoning up the probation officer and asking permission. If he wants to go abroad, God help him. Everything has to be sent in triplicate to the Home Office, and back, no less. I thought it would be nice just to have a trip to France; initially I thought of a day's shopping trip. It turned into a complete fiasco. By the time we had asked permission of everybody up to the Home Office and back the spontaneity was stone dead. He can also never emigrate: they turn down lifers who want to work abroad. Yet there is no work in this country for them. If he wanted to go to Scotland and do some work he would have to have another probation officer up there to see him. He is never free; they are never off his back, one way or another.

He has tried to get work, but it is impossible. He fills in the form and by the time he has admitted who he is and what he has done they either do not want to know or they only want to interview him because they want to find out what a real murderer looks like and whether they are the same as how they are portrayed on television. They want to know the ins and outs of the prison system. They have no intention of giving him the job. It is idle curiosity. Who wants to sit under a microscope every day of the week? It is no joke.

It is not just that he cannot get a job because there are millions of people unemployed; it is worse for him because of his record. It is a non-starting situation. I don't see him getting out of it. The only job he was offered was working at the bird sanctuary, where he would have had to live in a caravan. It had to be a live-in job, on £40 a week. Now that is going to be great, two kids and a wife on £40 a week. Can you imagine two teenage boys in a caravan? They would have had to send me to the funny farm. It doesn't do much for his self-esteem.

When lifers who are out are met with this barrage – not

being able to get a job, being looked at under a microscope – it takes away their self-esteem and their pride. It drags them further and further down. And then when they, out of despair, do something silly and they are back inside everybody says: 'I told you he was no good. What do you expect? He's an ex-con.' And these are the very people who put him under the microscope in the first place. Not that many years ago they were hanging people for murder. Then it was all swept under the carpet, neat and tidy. Now they are out in society and people don't like it. They feel uneasy, uncomfortable. It is temporary, until they get to know them, but initially they are wary. Being a life sentence prisoner can range from Barry's case to being a terrorist or to the Sutcliffes of this world. They are all put in the one bracket. It is ludicrous. In France they have crime of passion – not in this country. So is a crime of passion just as bad as being a terrorist? Is this what society is telling us? That is what I am hearing and I don't like it. I don't like it at all. I feel very angry.

In spite of everything I do love him to bits. I am 100 per cent committed and he knows it. I am much happier now than I was. My life has never been empty but I have wanted to have somebody to share it with. Life can be very sweet; you do not have to have pots of money, posh cars and luxury houses to live in. I take my pleasures in the simple things. I love flowers and nature and that is one thing we share. Because of his love of birds Barry has started breeding budgies. He has three beautiful little baby budgies hatched out. They are really gorgeous. Watching them grow is lovely. It gives a lot back. He is hoping to move on to macaws, but of course they are expensive to start off.

It is a case of one step at a time, really. I think if, along with the rest of the country, we can ride this recession and he is lucky enough to get a job then things would obviously take off. Things are taking off for him in a small way at the moment, which is not a bad thing. It is better to build up gradually than jump in two feet first and wonder what the hell you are doing. Things are coming together.

The difference in my life now is that I have somebody special for me, whereas before it was give, give, give, all the time to the boys. Every mother knows that, yes, you do get feedback, but you also give a hell of a lot and at the end of the day you do feel drained. It is really nice to have somebody there to share with, to share responsibilities as well. My younger son, being the way he is, can never be left on his own, so it is nice for me to hand over to Barry and say: 'I'm going out this evening.'

Sometimes now I can do the things I want to do and know that David is going to be well looked after and safe. It is great. Barry takes 90 per cent of the stress level of dealing with the college that David goes to, because David is a little tinker, to put it mildly. Because of where Barry has been he knows how men's minds work backwards. He knows what the boys are going to say before they have said it; he knows what stunts they are going to pull and he knows ways of catching them out, to show them where they are going wrong, rather than turning round and punching them. He deals with that side of things and he has a very good relationship with David's teacher. If there are any problems which need to be sorted out, I know Barry can do it. I sort out the financial side. I deal with the money and bills and Barry leaves me to do that. It is taking off pressure. I think that is part of what our marriage is about, the sharing.

It would have been easier if he had not been a lifer. We could go where we want when we wanted. He would not have to be worried that if he steps out of line he will be straight back in prison, no question about it – and we do not know how long for, because it is at the Home Office's discretion. I feel that once lifers have done their prison sentence it should be left, finished. He also should not have to declare it; he has paid it. You have got to give people a chance; you have got to try, and society is not prepared to do that.

Jane Officer

As a woman committed to the abolition of capital punishment, Jane Officer began writing to a prisoner, Andrew Lee Jones, on Death Row in Louisiana to try to relieve his loneliness. Death Row prisoners are kept in solitary confinement 23 hours a day, and can wait years for their execution. Like many people who write to men on Death Row who are members of Life Lines, Jane found herself involved with the prisoner as she almost literally became his lifeline, the only person he could talk to. After he was executed she took on another condemned man and became the co-ordinator for Life Lines in Louisiana. She helps organise letter-writing and also actively campaigns against the death penalty in the United States, liaising with opponents there. She has also set up a memorial fund for Andrew, which provides grants for people studying law in the United States who intend to defend people faced with the death penalty.

I was put in touch with Jane by a journalist who is on the board of Andrew's memorial fund. Jane met me at Birmingham railway station and took me to her home in a city suburb, which she shares with her cats. She is a widow and her children have left home. Jane is an advisory teacher for children with special needs and had had a tough day. When she talked about her impending retirement it was difficult to believe she was 58, as she looked ten years younger.

The starting point was seeing Paul Hamman's film *Fourteen Days in May* about the execution of Edward Earl Johnson in 1988. Then in May 1990 I read an article in the

Observer about Life Lines, a group of people who had seen the film and who were writing to people on Death Row in America.

I was very interested for several reasons. It was an opportunity to respond to that awful programme. Secondly, as I have worked a lot with very disturbed children, I thought there but for the grace of God go one of mine. I also decided to write because of the sheer loneliness of those men: they literally spend years in solitary confinement.

I was given the name of Andrew Lee Jones, who was in the Angola State Penitentiary in Louisiana. The names of the guys on Death Row were collected by the National Organisation Against the Death Penalty in the States, and one had been picked off the list and sent to me.

The first letter was quite easy to write because I decided it would just be a fairly short, introductory letter. However, I hesitated and walked around for a little while after I had written it, wondering whether to pop it in the post, because I realised that if I did get a response there was no going back on it. I wouldn't then be able to withdraw from the correspondence.

I had a reply within ten days, which was almost an immediate turnaround, since it takes about three or four days for post to get to and from America. Andrew wrote back saying he was so surprised because he was not expecting a letter from England. Now the situation is very different because the prisoners all know about Life Lines. When I opened the letter I realised this was a real person, not just a name and number any longer. Andrew told me a bit about himself and said he had been on Death Row since November 1984, but he did not tell me what he had done to be put there. One of the things we say at Life Lines is that we give unconditional support, regardless of what the prisoners have done. He did say in that very first letter: 'Feel free to ask me any questions that you want.'

I wrote back the same day and said I was very pleased

that he felt he wanted to write to me. I told him a bit more about me and my family to put myself into context and I wrote: 'If you would like to tell me about the crime you committed, I just want to make it clear right from the start that it won't make any difference. I won't stop writing to you if it is shocking.'

He did not tell me all in one go; it came out in bits of letters. He was very honest, particularly considering what the crime was. He was accused of breaking into the house of his ex-girlfriend, kidnapping her eleven-year-old daughter, then raping and murdering her and dumping her in a canal outside Baton Rouge. He was drunk at the time and has no recollection of that night at all.

In the letter in which he described it, he said he hoped I would feel OK about it. I wrote back and told him it was a dreadful crime but I had said I would write to him, and if he wanted to talk more about it then that was fine, I was quite happy to talk about it. After that we did not talk very much about why he was in Angola because we were, if you like, on a different plane. Our world became, as much as anything, me talking about what I did in my life, describing it in detail; all the little things which you would never say to friends. In prison people become extremely good at visualisation. It is a psychological way of lifting themselves out of that situation. Andrew was particularly good at that. He used to love me to give him really detailed descriptions of things that I had done and places I went to. An example would be that on a Saturday morning I would be in the dining room having a cup of coffee and I would say: 'I'm sitting here with a cup of coffee.' I would often even draw a little cup of coffee. I would tell him about the nitty-gritty details of my life. It is those little details which are so important to men like Andrew who are on Death Row.

He had a relationship with a young black woman, Euridell, who started writing to him from one of the Baptist churches in Freeport. She was visiting him when she could. They were obviously in love with one another. I became a mother confessor in a way, so he would talk to me when

Euridell had not written. He would worry that she had met somebody else. He wrote diaries about the routine of life in the prison: what was happening with other people in the prison, the day-to-day life and how hard people were being. He sent me all his diaries.

He did not write long letters because he did not have a great education, but some letters were really quite profound about the way that he looked on life.

A few months into writing, he told me about when he had received my first letter. He had not opened it straight away. He had taken it out in the hall with him for his recreation hour. They are locked up for 23 hours a day with an hour out, which is for showering and making phone calls. Out in the hall he had finally decided to open it. It had never struck me that he might not want to open it. He had been worried that he was not only getting hate mail from America, but from England as well. He said it was such a relief to open it and find it was not like that.

He would say how worried he was about having lost touch with his family. They lived only twenty miles away, but his mother did not visit him. He was quite clear about her reasons for not visiting.

He would talk about his fears of being executed. Although he was not religious, he was terrified of being buried in Angola, because he felt that if his body were buried there, his spirit would be imprisoned. I wrote back and said: 'Never worry about that. Whatever happens, even if there's nobody around, I'll make sure that you have a burial outside the prison.'

Then there was a turning-point. On New Year's Day 1991, he was given an execution date for early February. He wrote immediately to tell me about it. Reading the letter just turned my stomach over. I felt that this was the moment to make sure he had my telephone number, so I wrote giving it to him and explaining about the time difference.

The first time he rang it was actually two o'clock in the morning, because they do not have regular exercise times and he had to telephone during the hour he was allowed out of the cell. I just fell down the stairs, as we all do when we get phone calls in the middle of the night, worried that something had happened to a relative. This voice came over the phone and said in a deep Southern accent, 'Will you take this phone call from Andrew Lee Jones?' I had said, when I wrote, that he could reverse the charges because they were only allowed to make local calls from the telephone boxes.

He came on the phone and said: 'How are you doing?' I was talking quite fast, on an impulse to get in as much as I could in a short space of time. I said: 'How are you feeling?' He said: 'Very nervous.' I said: 'You're not nervous talking to me, we have been writing all this time.' But it was not talking to me: his problem was that he had four guards round him, as if he was going to go anywhere. He also had shackles and handcuffs on, which was part of the punishment. So it was nice, but a bit stilted because of that.

He had rung to tell me that he had a stay of execution on the grounds that the governor, who has to be in the state when an execution takes place, as he's the one responsible for whether it goes ahead or not, was going to be out of state in mid-February. Andrew had been constantly writing in his letters that what he wanted more than anything else was to 'set down', as he put it, and have a conversation with me. So I decided there and then that I would go and visit. It was a way of offering hope. I promised I would see him and wrote: 'If you can hang on until the summer I'll be there.' It was almost me saying: 'You've got to hang on, you've got to still be there.' I knew I could not get there before the summer because of school work.

He was thrilled about my promise but it also unleashed something in him. Round about that time, before he had his date lifted, I received a scribbled note written while he was in what they call 'the hole'. Understandably, when the people on Death Row have an execution date they are on a very short fuse and the slightest thing will upset them. He was put in the hole for ten days for some minor infringement.

He wrote me another letter from in there which was one of the most pathetic and sad I have ever received. It was cold and he was in there with only his tracksuit and a T-shirt. All his underwear was taken away, as well as his shoes and his socks. He was freezing. He had a blanket, but the rules said that you could not wrap the blanket round you until after dark. You had to sit there all day, just like that. With difficulty he managed to tear up his T-shirt and wrap it round his feet because they were so cold. He said the worst thing was 'I keep thinking that letters are coming from you and I can't read them. I can only scribble this note to you to say please carry on writing until I get out.'

When I got this letter I rang Amnesty, but they said there was nothing they could do. They cannot touch what is going on inside prisons.

I wrote several long letters, one of them specifically telling him that he was part of my family, like an eldest son. I said that a mother is not concerned about what her children have done, she would still love them whatever. I felt sure that if he could put his hands out to his real mum, if he could make a move, then there would be some response. I wrote this long letter about it and I had such a lovely letter back, in which he said that when he read mine he just sat and cried, and he had never cried the whole time he had been in Angola. It brought us much closer together. He said he knew it was now up to him to get hold of his mother.

In the course of time he had developed a shell and our relationship had, during this period, begun to knock chips in it. Being in the hole, having an execution date, sending the letter to me about his family and getting my response had meant that the whole protective layer had begun to collapse and he felt he was ready to reach out and make contact.

He asked me if I would write to his mother. I did and she replied with a very short note – because she can hardly write – but it was a lovely little letter, in which she said it was wonderful to know somebody cared about her son and how heartbroken she was. Just before Christmas the previous year her eldest daughter had been murdered by her son-in-law in a row over drugs. She was devastated by the loss as well as having Andrew facing execution.

His letters began to change: he had always signed them 'Peace and Friendship' at the end, but he changed it to 'Love'. During the time the execution date was hanging over him, I had been in the habit of writing a letter every day. It might have only been a card with a short note, but I never knew if this was going to be the last so I just carried on sending them.

Andrew became in my mind an amalgam of all sorts of people I had known, a mixture of the kids I had worked with and very much part of my family. He had started asking about my children and my life: 'What's Caroline been doing? Have you heard from David? How are the cats?' Sometimes Caroline or some of my friends would drop him a card. For people on Death Row there is a heightened sense that for them life has closed down as far as social relationships are concerned, so they channel their feelings into somebody else's family. Since Andrew had not been having contact with his own family, he became a surrogate son.

We had become close like a mother and son. In his letters he would sometimes slip in things like: 'I sometimes feel I'm breaking my code in telling you so much about myself but . . .' revealing something he had probably never told anyone else before. There was obviously a thought every now and then of how far can I trust this person? Will she use this information against me? By February it became clear that he trusted this woman who was writing to him from England.

Quite a number of the men on Death Row feel it is easier to trust us over here in Britain because we do not have the same connections. Some of them write to us and say: 'Can you find me someone over there who I can talk to? I cannot talk to anybody in this country, because they might use

125

it against me.' I understand that. We are also fortunate in that we don't have all the media bits that go with it. There is no way I would want to write to the Yorkshire Ripper, but that is mostly coloured by the fact that I have read all about him in the papers. Of course, there are bound to be people like that on Death Row who have got penfriends. It is entirely up to them to tell us what their crimes are. I have had people ringing me saying: 'How do you know if they're telling the truth?' I tell them: 'I don't.'

Andrew wrote me a long letter about how he felt that his family avoided contact because they blamed him for the fact that his older brother had been beaten up by the police. His brother had never been in trouble. Andrew said his brother had been taken in by the police and beaten up with a baseball bat to force him to say that Andrew had not been with him the night of the murder, when in fact he had. They had been drinking in a bar, which was where he had got drunk. Andrew felt he ought to be doing something about this but he was unable to, and he hated having to rely on other people to do it.

I had contacted the Death Penalty Resource Center in New Orleans. They have the most up-to-date information and are extremely helpful. When he was given the February execution date they had asked me if I would send a letter as a character witness for Andrew.

In the spring he wrote to tell me he had been given another execution date. It is awful what they do. They gave him two, which they changed quite quickly, in June, first the beginning then the end of the month. I was really worried. I was in Tyree, in Scotland, on holiday and I rang to find out what was happening. I said there was no way I could get out there before the end of July. The two dates were put off for technical reasons of various sorts but they gave him another, 22 July 1991.

Our letters were a mixture of fear and anxiety about what might or might not happen, but also, particularly from Andrew's point of view, excitement that 'we'll get to set down' and we'll get to do this or that. There was even a little sad bit where he said: 'If I'm actually on Death Watch it will be better, because we can have contact visits. You don't get them otherwise.' Even during the awful, really awful bit he was doing that.

In the meantime his mum and his sisters had been to visit, which was really wonderful. It was hard for everybody, because they were in tears and he had to control himself. His mum cried the whole time. It was hard for them to visit; it is hard for anybody because there's a metal screen between the prisoner and the visitor which literally has just a few pinholes in it. It is not even a glass screen. Even in that situation the prisoner's wrists are handcuffed and their ankles are shackled together. They also have a 'black box' on the handcuffs' chain to prevent them moving their hands. They cannot sit down for long because their hands are at an awkward angle, so they have to stand up because it is too uncomfortable to sit with their hands like that.

He rang me a couple more times, the first time at nine o'clock in the evening. He said: 'Oh, your voice sounds different.' I said: 'Yeah, it does sound different because the last time you rang it was two o'clock in the morning and you woke me up, so I had just come down from sleep.' He was fascinated, as you might imagine, by 'that English accent'. He had never heard anybody speak with an English accent. We had this joke because I said: 'I'm the one who speaks properly, you're the one with an accent.' We gradually moved towards the plans that I was making to go over there and the strong desire he had 'to set down' and talk about things.

One of Caroline's friends did a bit for the *Birmingham Post* and I sent him a copy. He could not believe that he was being presented in a positive light. It was a totally new experience after what had happened to him. As well as the article there was a photograph of him smiling with his handcuffs on.

He wrote poems, which were not specifically for me, but about his situation. He used me a lot as his sounding-board for various things. He would say that I had come into his life at the right time when he had needed somebody. He had thought all he was ever going to hear for the rest of his life was prison talk, and he said it was wonderful to be able to talk about things which were to do with real life.

I sent him books, and he was over the moon. His favourite reading was cowboy books, so I got him a subscription to a magazine. The things they like best are postcards. Andrew's favourite book was one I sent him called *Journey Through Wales*: the photographs in it were beautiful, and there was very little text. He absolutely loved that book, and he would turn to it when he was writing to me and say: 'You know that one . . .' I would have to go into Dillons and check it out before I replied to his letter. One reason why this book was so special was because he had spent his whole life in the Mississippi Delta, where there are not even any hills, so the idea of mountains was a real treat.

I was concerned about the fact that the execution date was coming up before the end of term, but my boss allowed me to leave a week early. So I left for the United States in mid-July, accompanied by my friend Vi, who writes to a prisoner in Florida. Due to plane delays at Gatwick, instead of arriving at a reasonable hour we arrived at midnight their time. When we got out of the plane we were literally knocked back by the heat. We had never thought about that: it is not just hot, it is tropical. The temperature was 100 degrees with a humidity of 90 degrees. In this country the cold air hits you as you get off the plane; there it was totally the reverse, you are hit full in the face by damp heat and the sound of those cicadas.

We did not pick up the car that night, there was no way I was going to drive then because I was absolutely knackered. We went to stay at the hotel and first thing the next morning, after very little sleep, people were on the phone to us and we were ringing others. I spoke to Andrew's mother and to Carol Lang, his 'spiritual adviser'. Andrew had apparently been ringing everybody the night before to see when I would arrive and asking people to check every hotel in Baton Rouge to find out where I was. I had sort of known that I had a certain importance but in the course of the following days I realised how central I had become to him. Talking to his mum made me realise that making this journey for somebody who felt he was not worthy of anybody's time at all, gave all sorts of positive messages to people, particularly as I was white.

Prison visiting hours in the South are usually from about eight o'clock in the morning until about 3.30 p.m. You are allowed two hours. He wanted me to get up there as fast as possible, but Baton Rouge was 60 miles away from Angola Prison. I rushed to the airport to get the car so that we could make our way up there. We took a highway up into Mississippi and turned off down a long, narrow road which goes nowhere except to the prison, which was originally a slave plantation. It felt like being in the movies, going down this dirt track which was only partly made up, and then turning a bend and seeing a watchtower with somebody up there.

First we had to find somewhere for Vi to go, because she could not sit in the car – she would have been roasted alive. Directly outside the prison gates was a building which could have come out of the film *The Good, the Bad and the Ugly*. It was a wooden hut with a fan in it, which guards used when they were off duty. It had a pool table, a few old tables and not much else, but at least they sold drinks and the fan worked. That was about all it had going for it. It was run by somebody who was related to one of the warders. All these Southern prisons are run by nepotism. The warders are part of prison families and when the kids grow up they work in the prison too. There are some black guards, but the majority are white and 80 per cent of the 5,000 prisoners are black. It is a long-term prison, and many of the men have been there for most of their lives.

I went to the Nissen huts and presented my pass. I was the first person to come from England to visit a prisoner on Death Row and they could not understand why I had come. The first gate was electronically opened and when it shut behind me I was totally struck by the most beautiful gardens tended by a young man. They were very formal, laid out with geraniums, marigolds and other classical flowers, and not a weed in sight. We walked down a path to Death Row. There was just a hall with a drinks machine and an office. I was struck immediately by the cleanliness of the place, but everything was hard – metal, concrete or brick. I was told I would have to wait because Andrew was seeing his solicitor and I sat there for about an hour and a half. One of the guards bought me a Coke because I had no money on me. I had not known until then that you are allowed to take $10 for the prisoner. The guards could not understand why I was there. They kept coming out and saying: 'Are you going to wait?'

'Yes.'

'But, ma'am, you've been here half an hour. I dunno, ma'am, I dunno why you don't go.'

I said: 'I've travelled five thousand miles to come here. What's an hour and a half?'

They kept thinking I would just give up and go. There were miniature mug shots of all the prisoners and I was looking at them, trying to make a mental note for the people who were writing to other men on Death Row in Angola, so that when I got home I would be able to say: 'I saw a photograph of your prisoner.' Like all mug shots they were awful. One would not want to be in a room with any of those men, the way they were depicted.

Finally, Andrew's solicitor, Michelle, came out. One of the things the Death Penalty Resource Center ensures is that the prisoner gets a local defence lawyer. Andrew had a Pardon Board hearing to try to stop the execution on the Friday, and she wanted me to speak at it. There was also a reporter, James Minton, the senior crime reporter of the *Morning Advocate*, the local newspaper in Baton Rouge who wanted to interview me. Michelle asked me if I would speak at the hearing. I said: 'I don't mind. You're the one who needs to say if it's OK, because you're Andrew's lawyer.'

Her answer sent a chill through my heart: 'Nothing can do him any harm at this stage.'

I went through a sliding door and the guard on the other side shouted: 'Woman on the floor.'

No man is allowed to be on the corridor when a woman walks through, and some prisoners were working in the kitchens. I did not realise that Andrew was actually already there, in a little cubicle. It was strange, obviously, but we knew one another and there were no difficult formalities. We were straight into: 'It's wonderful to see you,' and 'I wish I could see you.' I said that because I could barely see him through the pinholes in the metal – he was black against a black background. It was easier for him because the room I was in was light and I am white, so he could make me out. He did not want to talk about what was coming up.

He said: 'You do talk slow.'

'I don't talk slow, I know I don't.'

He said: 'Compared to the way you talked over the phone.'

I said: 'I've got time to talk, time for a dialogue, not like a transatlantic call where your voice breaks up and one voice cuts off the other.'

We had been talking for about an hour when the guard came up. James Minton, whom Michelle had mentioned earlier, but whom I had completely forgotten about, came in. He asked me if I would mind having some photographs taken with Andrew.

'Of course you can take some photographs, but it's pretty pointless. You can't even see Andrew, because of that screen.'

He replied: 'They won't allow me to have you two together so that I can take some photographs. They are saying no way, absolutely no way.'

It was wrong, because Andrew was on Death Watch the week prior to the execution, and he should have been allowed contact visits, but they make up the rules as they go along. James took some photographs of me and we carried on talking. Then he put his hand on my shoulder and said, 'Hang on a minute, I'll see what I can do.' He went out for a few minutes. Then the guard came in, beckoned me out and asked me to come into the office. I immediately thought: 'Oh God. Have I transgressed? Have I done something I shouldn't have?'

In the office James gave me this great big smile and winked when I went past him. He said quickly, 'I'll take as long as I can.'

He told me afterwards that the guards were not too bright and they had warned him that the pictures he had been taking were a waste of time because he would not be able to see anything. He had agreed with them, adding that he had come all this way and he couldn't get anything. And they said: 'Oh well, we'll see what we can do.'

They brought Andrew through, shackled and handcuffed and wearing this great big grin. I had been warned not to touch him or they would terminate the visit immediately. In the office there were two guards and James so, as you might imagine, it was quite difficult trying to have a conversation in there, but at least we laughed a lot. I shall never forget, because it was somewhat unnerving for me, how hard Andrew was concentrating on looking at me, particularly at my face. The only way I can describe it is to say that it was as if he was taking a million photographs over and over again. I could see this by the little flickers and movements of his eyes. It was almost as if he was trying to get a total picture of what I looked like and recording it in his mind to take back with him when he went.

When I visited him the next day, I commented on this saying: 'You really put me under the microscope. I hope it wasn't too difficult with all my lines.' And I laughed. From behind the screen, he described me in minute detail. I suppose when you are faced with that totally sterile situation and you have an opportunity to see someone that you have grown to love as a friend, you want to grasp it all and take it all in.

I did it too, to a lesser extent. I was certainly looking at him and commenting on things. He was very nervous. The nervousness was as much to do with being with the guards as being with me.

James kept us there for about fifteen minutes, as long as he could. He kept on saying: 'I'll take another one.'

'Can you take one of me, just on my own, so that I can give it to my mother?' Andrew asked.

Finally the guards called a halt to it. When Andrew stood up I just stroked my finger lightly down his forearm. It did not really matter at that stage, as the visit was coming to an end, and I could not stop myself. It really hurt that when he left and was led off, he had to shuffle. There is no other way of walking in shackles except by moving in tiny little steps. It was bad enough having to see him being taken away. I also found it hard that here was this healthy, strong young man behaving, like they all do, in a very submissive way, never making eye contact with the guards, always keeping his head and shoulders down.

James met up with Vi and me in the 'café' after I had had a discussion about coming the next day. The guard had said: 'No, you can't. You can only come twice a month.' I asked them if, as I had come all this way, I could have two visits together. They had to ring through to the warden's office to see if it was all right if I came again the following day. They had to make their little protest about it, but they finally agreed. One has to play along with the system, so I said: 'I'm so grateful to you. That's really nice of you. Thank you very much.'

I was thinking that it was not very nice at all.

In the café, James lifted our hopes. He said the general feeling was that they would not execute Andrew because they did not want to put anybody else in the electric chair. He thought the case would be deferred until a new bill came forward for lethal injection. I was quite heartened by that. We left and James said he would follow us to see that we were OK because the roads were so deserted.

When we got back to the hotel room, Andrew's spiritual adviser telephoned and said she was going up to stay by the prison on Sunday. I asked her why and she said it was for the execution. I wondered how a spiritual adviser could say this: we had not even had the Pardon Board hearing. She just said that he would be executed.

'How can you say that when there is still this major thing to go?'

She said: 'Andrew has to prepare to meet the Lord at one minute past midnight on Monday.'

I later realised that no one is employed as a spiritual adviser in the prison unless they believe in the death penalty. That was a stunner.

The next morning, Thursday, we went across the Mississippi to see Andrew's mother at her home. She was a big black mamma and just hugged me tight to show how important I was to her. I took the ferry from her place back to the prison. When I visited Andrew later that day, he was anxious but I can not remember what we talked about because it was all just ordinary chat.

There was a woman visiting one of the other prisoners, a man who had become a Muslim in prison. This dear old lady of about 80 was the only person who ever visited him. She was a devout Christian and would come up once a month to read him long tracts from the Bible. When, later, I wrote to him and asked about it, he said it was better than nothing. It was really awful for the poor man, his only conversation.

Andrew was clearly very anxious at this point and he could feel the vibes coming off me through the screen. I told him that we must carry on: we still had the Pardon Board hearing.

The Pardon Board hearing started at eight o'clock, early, like everything in prison, and went on for nine and a half hours. All Andrew's family had travelled to be there. He came from a big family, with sixteen brothers and sisters.

The hearing was inside the prison, about five miles from the gate, in the building next to the Death House. I think they allowed him to leave his handcuffs off, but he still wore his shackles. It was weird because the room was used as a lecture room and to have meetings in. The arrangement was a bit like a wedding: people on the left were those for the prosecution; people on the right were with the defence and the five at the front were the Pardon Board. There were also television cameras, radio, reporters and the rest of the media. I had not understood this and sat down on the prosecution side, then realised, once it had started, that I had to get over to the defence side without being too obvious. I was sitting directly behind some policemen who were making remarks like: 'This is all a waste of time. Why don't we get on and kill him?'

Then I met Carol Lang, the spiritual adviser, in person for the first time and she and I took an immediate dislike to one another. She was one of those skinny, tight-lipped American women. One reason why she had taken against me was that she had asked Andrew what I was like and he had told her that I was a lovely little white-haired old lady who could barely walk by herself. He was joking with her, and she was clearly most annoyed that I did not fit that description. It annoyed her because when he had been talking with a great deal of affection about me, it was OK because I was supposed to be grandmotherly. But I was not, and people are funny about these things.

When the Pardon Board hearing started I spoke first. I am used to talking in public, as training people and talking to groups is part of my job, but I had only five minutes. Five minutes to say what you think about a person when their life can literally depend on it is a different sort of thing altogether. It was very hard to keep my voice steady and I don't think I did. I had to keep brushing the tears away. I told them what I believed: that the person they had here was not the person who had been locked up seven years before in 1984. He had told me so many times that he would dearly love the chance to make up for any of the wrongs he had done. I said that if they executed him they were taking away the opportunity for him to make atonement: 'You just go on and produce more victims. His family will become victims if you do this.' I did not say 'of murder', but 'of another death'.

Then we had a long session. The defence called both a psychologist and a psychiatrist. I had been warned that they would talk about Andrew suffering from schizophrenia or brain damage, because those are two of the only defences they have, so they use them even if it is not true.

Andrew's mother then took the stand and that was awful because, for the first time, I heard a long catalogue of the awfulness of their lives. One imagines that the days of slavery are gone, but what has replaced them is not much better. The first thing you are struck by in Louisiana is that you don't see mixed couples. People are still segregated.

Andrew was the eldest child of his mother's second marriage. Her first husband had died and altogether she had had seventeen children. They had lived on a plantation just the other side of the Mississippi River where they were sharecroppers. They were allowed to have a little land of their own to grow vegetables as long as any money that they earned was spent at the plantation store. They could not buy food from anywhere else. Andrew's father was the chauffeur for the people who owned the plantation. He developed cancer, but was not allowed to go to hospital. He just carried on working. Obviously, they had no insurance. This was not a long time ago – we are talking about the late 1960s. Andrew was sixteen when his father died. He was with him at the end and was absolutely distraught. He was totally devoted to his father. Andrew described him as a loving man who adored his children, took them places and never hit them.

In the way that teenagers do if something traumatic like that happens, he dropped out. He had gone off into Baton Rouge and joined the kids on the street. Then he had the most unfortunate luck: he had never been involved with the police, but he was caught pinching a six-pack of beer from the store, for which, at the age of eighteen, he was given a sentence of ten years in Angola. As a teenager he was put in a jail that is notorious for being the worst in the United States.

When he came out he got involved with a girl who really manipulated him: she was obviously a lot brighter than he and she had a drug habit, while he was a home boy with little idea of anything.

Meanwhile, his family had had the most dreadful time. As soon as the father died, they had been thrown off the plantation and had nowhere to live. They had finally managed to get a little place.

At the Pardon Board they asked Andrew's mother why she had not had family counselling. It was ridiculous: they did not seem to understand that she barely had enough money for food, let alone counselling. Everyone said what a lovely boy he was until he became involved with this particular girl.

This went on all day with a lot of defence witnesses. They did not need a prosecution witness: the district attorney got up and said: 'That nigger over there. He ain't fit to walk on this earth.' They also brought in the step-grandfather of the girl who had been murdered. All he had to do was to stand up and say: 'I want that nigger dead,' and that was it.

The board went out and then there was the awful waiting. When they came back they said that the two black people on the Pardon Board wanted the sentence commuted to life, while the two white people voted for death but wanted to delay it until the lethal injection became the penalty. The black woman who chaired the Pardon Board hearing came down on death by lethal injection. I thought this meant we had a bit of hope, but I could tell by the lawyers' faces it did not. The governor was not going to delay executing him this weekend as he was against the idea of bringing in lethal injection at this point and had an election to win.

When they announced the result, pandemonium broke out. Then, before we knew it, Andrew was whisked away and no one was able to say goodbye to him. Five guards came and literally lifted him up, taking him out by the side door, and threw him into a police car. He was taken straight back to Death Row. We were told afterwards that when he got there he went absolutely berserk, and was afterwards told that he was not going to be allowed to have any visitors at all before his execution.

Nick Trenticosta, the director of the Death Penalty Resource Center, had an argument with them, saying he would blow the whole thing wide open if they did not allow Andrew to have visitors. He would talk to the press. He made a bargain with them: he would not set foot in Angola for the next six months if they would allow Andrew to have visitors.

The lawyers and I were outside waiting for the fleet of minibuses to take us back up to the gate. We just stood in a circle with our arms round one another and we all cried, even the men. For the lawyers it was worse because they had fought and fought, working 24 hours a day for weeks on end trying to find an issue for a reprieve. Now they knew they would have to work for the whole weekend, trying to get to the Supreme Court in Washington and go through all that. We all went up to the gate and stood there. I remember Michelle, his defence lawyer, saying: 'We will win the fight against the death penalty. I am certain we shall win it. But whether it will be in my lifetime I doubt. We can't allow this awfulness to go on.'

When they went off, I went to collect Vi, who had been waiting all the time in the café. It had been so awful in there that she had considered going out and sitting in the heat. The men inside had been saying: 'We should just clear all the trash out. Kill them all in one go,' and awful things like that. She found it very offensive but she had no choice but to carry on sitting there.

We went back to the hotel and rang Andrew's family to see how they were. At eleven o'clock Sarah Ottinger, a lawyer at the Resource Center, rang from New Orleans. She said: 'It really is going to go ahead, I'm afraid. There isn't anything we can do to stop it.' I was just shaking all over and did not sleep that night.

The next day, Saturday, Vi and I had planned to move

up to a beautiful little town which was only about twenty miles from the prison. That was a weird experience, because it was a holiday area and everybody else was going out hunting, shooting and fishing, while we did not dare to move out of our room, not even to eat. We used the room service. If a phone call came through, we wanted to make sure we were there. It was just a question of waiting.

On the Sunday I was feeling dreadful. At about twelve o'clock the phone rang. It was Neil Walker from the Resource Center, who said: 'How fast can you move up to Angola?'

'I can be there in twenty minutes if I break all the speed limits.'

'Right. Go. Andrew wants you to be there with his family.'

I just picked up my papers and car keys, told Vi she did not have to come, and flew out.

The family were gathered around a table which had a cloth on it. It was almost like the Last Supper, with Andrew on the right-hand side. His mother was sitting beside him and Euridell, his girlfriend, was there. It was the first time I had met her. It was also the first time they had ever been able to meet properly, and see each other. I put my arms round him and hugged him. He whispered in my ear: 'This is Euridell.' For about three or four minutes the three of us just stood there clinging to each other.

Then I talked to the other people there. The men were finding it much more difficult to cope with. People started saying goodbye and leaving. In the end all the people remaining were the women in the family, plus Euridell and me. The others went off to the gate where they waited and cried. It was about one o'clock and we were told that we were allowed to stay until six. There were occasional prayers and some crying and wailing, but also a lot of laughs. Carolyn, Andrew's sister, a lovely girl, would say: 'Do you remember when we did this?' or 'Do you remember when we did that?' I realised that in their holiday times and weekends and evenings, they were expected to work, either picking cotton or corn for nothing or on some other task for the plantation owner. They were talking about practical jokes they used to play, like putting firecrackers in the post box. Then the conversation would go down and there would be a pool of silence.

The guards were preparing the electric chair. We knew that because the lights kept dimming. Someone came in and offered Andrew some food, but he couldn't eat it.

Andrew had told Debra, one of the lawyers, that once a year there was a religious seminar in Angola and it was the only time when Death Row prisoners were allowed to be together for a day. He said that he enjoyed the seminar, but could not eat with the others because he had spent so many years eating on his own in his cell that he couldn't eat with other people any more. I gather it happens to quite a lot of solitary prisoners – they cannot deal with social eating.

All the time I could see the terror in his eyes. They were all bloodshot and he was consciously aware all the time of who was coming and going. Despite the fact that there was some laughing, there was really absolute terror and fear. His mouth was dry and he tried to drink a Coke, but it did not help.

Somebody came in with a message to say the governor had turned down his appeal and the only thing they had left was the Supreme Court in Washington, which generally does not rule until about half an hour before the execution.

At about a quarter to six, the warden of Angola came in, a tall man wearing a Stetson and cowboy boots, and said it was time for everybody to go because they had to prepare the prisoner. I tried to make a point of saying goodbye first and leaving because I thought it was only right that his family should have the opportunity to be alone with him. So I went over and hugged him. He whispered: 'Don't let anybody cry until they leave the building. I couldn't cope if they did that.' So I said that we would do the best we could. I also told him I loved him and what a privilege it was to be his friend.

Earlier his mother had asked me to go into the toilet with her as she wanted to speak to me. She wanted me to go with her after the execution to the funeral parlour and look at her son's body to see what they had done to it. I told her I would certainly do that and, with her permission, I would like to bring a camera and take photographs. She agreed, saying: 'I want everybody to know what an electrocution does to people.' I thought that was an amazingly brave thing for a mother to say.

We got to the point of saying our goodbyes and everybody kept themselves together. It was very good, really, in the circumstances, even though there was a feeling of unreality throughout.

Then the spiritual advisers arrived. Andrew's mum commented: 'They send four spiritual advisers and not one of them is black.' One of them was Carol Lang, and she looked at me malevolently because she had told me at the end of the Pardon Board hearing that I had been too late to say goodbye to Andrew.

The last person to leave was his mother. We were on the other side of the screen by this time and Carolyn kept saying: 'Don't let any of those guards see us cry. Don't let them have that pleasure.'

His mother's final task was to watch Andrew sign his body over to her and she had to sign to receive it. We watched them doing this through the glass. She came through and we all stood there, on the other side of that glass wall, waving and cheering. We told him to keep going, and shouted, 'It's not over until it's over.' Finally we were pushed out of the door into the yard. We tried terribly hard to control ourselves but we all fell on one another in tears. It was terrible. Just before we left, we were given all Andrew's possessions. This probably triggered it off. All his worldly belongings went in one disposable blanket, which was tied in a knot at the top, and one paper bag, like those you get from a store.

When we got to the gate we met up with the men. By this time it was about a quarter past six. We arranged that

I would go back and collect Vi and we would catch the ferry across the Mississippi to go down to their house and wait with them.

It was an amazing experience. There was a tremendous amount of support from relatives and friends. People came from all over to be with them, which I thought was really something. The men, without exception, all got very, very drunk. The daughters of the family cooked this wonderful meal, but I am a vegetarian and all Cajun Creole food is very meat-orientated. It was that night which convinced me I really was a vegetarian. Of course, it was partly to do with the occasion, but I found the whole texture and taste appalling.

We had the television on to keep up with events. From nine o'clock the telephone was ringing continuously because Andrew was allowed free calls and we were all talking to him. He managed to say goodbye to all his brothers and sisters.

Then I heard his mum let out this most awful wail. I'll never forget it. He had just got the message that the Supreme Court had turned him down. One of Andrew's younger brothers was on the sofa with his head on my lap. He was very, very drunk and he was crying his heart out, saying how Andrew had always been his favourite brother and telling me how wonderful he was.

At 12.20 a.m. we got the message that the execution had gone ahead.

I sat on the stoop from about six in the morning with Velma, Andrew's closest sister, and talked of the family and the event. At about eight Andrew's mum rang the funeral parlour to arrange for us to view the body. They told her that she should not see the body because she would find the smell offensive. We tried to puzzle out what this might mean and I still do not know whether it was the smell of burning or the formaldehyde which they put in dead bodies which they thought would worry us. They refused to let us come, and we tried again at twelve but they said no again, because they were preparing the body. They should never have done this, but it was quite clear that somebody had said that we were not allowed to go and see the body before it had been dealt with. We both felt that he had been badly mutilated. I have seen photographs of what has happened in that chair and it is dreadful. It is one of the reasons why they are changing from the electric chair to lethal injection. According to the press reports, it took about seventeen minutes for Andrew to die.

We drove down to the funeral parlour, which was in Port Allen. It had a florist attached and I said I wanted some flowers for Andrew. I got this sidelong look and was asked if that was the man who had been executed that morning. I said yes, and asked if it was possible for me to see him to say goodbye. They looked askance and said no. I said he was a friend of mine and I would like to pay my last respects, but I never managed to. I just bought some flowers and left them there, because I knew I would not be able to go to the funeral.

By then Vi and I both felt it was the right time to go. We had done what we could to support them. We had fulfilled our reason for going and the family grief was now for them to deal with: if they had to worry about us as well, we would be making it more difficult for them.

We had always planned to go on to Florida and meet people there and to visit the Death Penalty Resource Center in Tallahassee to meet a prominent defence lawyer.

When we returned to Britain it was like coming back to another life, although we had been away for less than a fortnight. I was surprised to find a letter from Andrew waiting for me, which he had written on the night of the Pardon Board hearing. He thanked me for everything I had done and said I had come into his life at the right time. I felt he was talking about how he had been able to make peace with his family. He said the most difficult part for him was hurting other people by going to his death this way. He wanted me to know how much it had meant to him that I came over and also how important it was that everybody had sent their prayers and their cards. He said that he did not go to his grave feeling any ill will towards anyone. He was emotionally tired and had come to the stage where he did not want any more reprieves. One can imagine what he had been through: he had had ten execution dates. He said: 'I want them to do it this time, I can't go on like this.'

I still find it very difficult to come to terms with the process: the state actually making a conscious decision to take the life of someone who is young and strong. One can cope with people dying – I have been through that with people – but to set about a cold-blooded procedure to take a person's life is terrible, regardless of what they have done.

I just keep remembering what a lovely person he was. In some ways it would be easier if I heard that he was dreadful, but everything I keep hearing, in dribs and drabs, even now, is about what a nice person he was and what a bad break he had and how he was never defended properly.

Andrew Lee Jones Fund, 1 Hemyock Road, Selly Oak, Birmingham B29 4DG. Tel: 021 475 4344.

Part 3

Mothers, Daughters and Sisters

This is perhaps the saddest group of women. For them, the killings came as a bolt from the blue and tore their lives apart, forcing them to question everything they had taken for granted.

Sara, whose brother killed his wife, had to deal with the crime in the most practical way. She took in his three-year-old boy, who had been left in the house with his dead mother and was, understandably, deeply traumatised. His demands on her were so great that she had to take time off work and lost the only well-paid job she had had. When she had managed to sort out the little boy, her brother was suddenly let out of jail and came to live with her too, causing havoc.

Yet, because she has a husband and daughter who are the primary focus of her life, and the boy has become like a child of hers, in the end she will probably be the least affected.

Susan has a father who still refuses to admit that he killed her mother and who is now vilified by the rest of her family. She too has a family of her own, but the killing of one of her parents by the other has removed stability from her life. She wants to believe her father innocent, yet knows that he did it. She loves him, yet finds his crime unforgivable. She is her father's lifeline and understands that he worries that if he told her the truth he would lose her as well, yet she longs for the truth so that together they can come to terms with what he did.

Ruth and Theresa discovered that their sons had murdered and neither of them will ever get over it. For both of them it was a drawn-out process because their sons began by denying it. When they finally confessed it was not the jail sentence which worried them, but that their families would be so appalled by what they had done that they would be abandoned. While Ruth and Theresa have come to terms with their sons' crimes, they are the sort of mothers who would have supported their sons however evil the deed. Joan told me that James was her son, no matter what he had done.

These are mothers who know their sons have committed the ultimate crime and will have to live with it for the rest of their lives.

Sara

When her brother killed his wife, Sara took in their three-year-old son, Andrew. He had been left in the house with his dead mother before the police arrived. Sara made Andrew part of her family but his demands put a strain on her marriage and her daughter and lost her the first well-paid job she had held since becoming a mother. She is a dynamic woman in her mid-thirties who is used to making things happen rather than patiently waiting for life to come right. Her marriage and family survived the onslaught of the traumatised child, who still lives with them in their detached house in Glasgow. Her husband, Martin, is an engineer working on computers. She works part-time in an estate office in the town.

I was the eldest of five children, three girls and two boys. Peter is the third child. We were all brought up in Scotland. My parents are divorced and the family was never particularly close – we used to see each other fairly often, but we had our own lives to live.

When I left school, I joined the Army and moved away from Scotland. But I married a policeman and, to my horror, he was posted to Glasgow, so we came back. We split up a few years later, but as I had my daughter, Emily, and my family lived here, it seemed better to stay.

I met Martin about two and a half years later. He moved in with us, then we decided to make it official and we have been married about five years.

My brother Peter married Clare after I returned to Glasgow. Nobody was invited to the wedding because it was a spur-of-the-moment decision and we did not know about it, which is typical of Peter. I never got to know her particularly well, but I liked her and she fitted into the family. When she had their son, Andrew, we all went to his christening and shortly afterwards they came to my second wedding. From the outside Peter and Clare's marriage seemed great. Nobody knew what went on when they were alone, but as far as I could see, it was all right until about a year before she was killed. Clare had an abortion and after that everything started going downhill. Her doctor pinpoints that event as the turning-point as apparently it affects some women like that. She became very depressed and started saying that she wanted Andrew but not Peter. She wanted the house, but not with Peter in it. Peter had never wanted Clare to have the abortion but she had gone ahead anyway. After that, Peter found her so difficult that he started getting depressed as well, because he did not want to leave her and she just wanted him out of her life. He tried talking to her about what was going wrong, but she did not want to know and just told him to go. He talked to the family about it and came to both me and my sister Susan's house, where my mum lived, several times a week.

Clare kept on threatening to take Andrew away from Peter for good. Andrew was three years old and the lawyer said she could not stop him from seeing his son because he had to have visiting rights. She said the solicitor could say what he liked but she would not give him visiting rights. She was going to take his son and not allow him any contact. Peter was very upset, because he and Andrew were always very close – kids are a big part of our family – and I think that was the final straw.

Peter came to see me two days before the killing and said Clare was still going to take Andrew away from him. He had been to his doctor and looked a mess, like an old man. He was seriously depressed and was on anti-depressants, and he was up one minute and down the next. He was not eating. The doctor said he was having a nervous breakdown. I told him to pull himself together and to go and speak to her again to get something sorted out. However, I did not have a lot of time for him that day. I was working in a clothes shop and even though I had only been there five months, I had just been promoted to assistant manager and I was trying to prove that I could do the job because it was a good opportunity for me. I could not deal with Peter in work time. When he came in to try to talk to me, I told him that he had to go because I was busy. I feel terribly guilty about not making the time to talk to him that day.

Two evenings later, at 7.30, Emily, Martin and I were watching television when I got a phone call. All I could hear was a woman screaming. I thought she said: 'Peter's killing Clare.' I found out later that it was my sister's next-door neighbour, who was trying to tell me that Peter had killed Clare and had run to my sister's house. He had run to Susan's looking for my mum, but she was in Wales, visiting my other sister, Julie.

Martin drove Emily and I down to Peter's house and when we got there I saw an ambulance pulling away. There were no sirens going so I realised she must be dead. We pulled up at the house and the police let me in but not Martin. They told me that my brother had killed his wife and was now missing.

We drove to where my mum and Susan lived and my sister was there in a distressed state because Peter had gone there covered in blood to tell her what he had done. The house does not have a telephone so I went next door to call my mum in Wales. I will never forget that phone call. I spoke to Anne first and then she put my mum on. I said to my mother: 'Peter has killed Clare.'

She told me not to be so stupid, and said that I was only having her on.

I told her I was not having her on, and we started screaming and crying at each other.

I did not have my dad's address or telephone number because we were not keeping in touch at the time. I had to go back to Peter's house and ask the police if I could go in to look for my dad's number. While I was there, they asked me what state of mind Peter was in, and if I thought he would top himself. I didn't want to have to think about it, but I said I did not have a clue. They gave me my dad's address and I had to go back to my mum's neighbour's house and phone him. He was crying on the phone.

Then I rang my other brother, and he said he did not believe me. He just said: 'I'll see you tomorrow.' I got Susan, locked up her house and took her back to mine. Then my other brother turned up at our house and I had to tell him about it.

All this time I did not feel anything, I just had to keep on dealing with different people. I desperately wanted to go and look for Peter to bring him home safely. I was worried about what he might do to himself. I thought about Clare briefly but, and I know this sounds awful, she was the least of my concerns at that time. I was also desperately worried about Andrew, who had been in the house when Peter killed Clare. They had taken him to the hospital.

That night my brother, sister, Martin and I all sat at my house and talked. We were all terribly worried about Peter because none of us had heard from him or knew where he was. Even though he had killed Clare, I did not want him to kill himself as well and I sensed he would not. My sister Susan thought he would. We could not stop crying. We drank a lot and smoked loads. It did not seem real – we could not believe that Peter had killed Clare. I never saw him as a murderer. It never crossed my mind that he had killed her on purpose. He obviously did it on the spur of the moment and did not mean to do it, I am sure of that.

We found out later what had happened. Clare had been out and when Peter saw her coming back all dressed up, he thought she was seeing someone else. We still do not know if she was or not. As she came in, there was a phone call and Peter went to answer it, but when he picked it up no one was there. They had an argument and Clare said that he should have let her answer it. The whole thing was over a bloody phone call. The argument got worse and there was a knife there which he picked up, and he stabbed her with it. He was hugging her all the time and she kept saying: 'Don't, Peter, don't.' Then she died. He was hugging her so much he fell on the floor with her. He had stabbed her eleven times, but afterwards he could not remember doing it. The doctor said it was a frenzied attack. Andrew came down and Peter ran out, closed all the doors, got into the car and drove to my sister's house.

After leaving my sister, he drove miles and miles out of Glasgow and smashed his car into a wall in an attempt to kill himself. He still has the gash on his head. Then he drove to the hospital and asked to see Clare. He knew he had hurt her, but he did not think that he had killed her. I think that was just to block out what he had done. The police arrested him at the hospital, but they never told us he had been found. The lawyers told us. The police never told us anything and we had to find it all out for ourselves.

They arrested him around four o'clock in the morning and took him to Glasgow's police station. I was up all night and we got a phone call at about six o'clock in the morning from Peter's solicitor telling us that he had been arrested. We went down to the police station and asked if we could see him, but we were refused. He was in the Magistrates' Court at nine o'clock, as soon as it opened. We went to the court and Peter came up from the cells in the clothes they had given him – paper trousers and paper jacket. He looked awful. I just wanted to get those horrible clothes off him. I know it sounds petty but I desperately wanted him in normal clothes. That was the first time we had seen him since it happened, but we were not allowed to talk to him. It seemed as if we were in there for about two seconds. He was remanded for a week, taken back down to the cells and we were told he was going to a Scottish jail.

My sister Julie had come over from Wales for the court hearing. She and I went to the jail and asked if we could see him. We were told we could but we would have to wait. We waited an hour and a half and then they told us that we could not see him as there had been a mix-up and we had to go home. The next day I returned to the prison with my dad and finally got to see Peter. We were allowed three-quarters of an hour to talk to him and it was a terrible visit. He had been in a prison cell for nearly two days and to look at him I could hardly see my brother. He looked old and depressed and he could not stop crying. He just kept holding me and kissing me, saying he was sorry and that he had not meant it to happen. He had thought that we would not want to know him after what he had done. He was still in shock and could not understand what he had done. I kept saying to him: 'Peter, you have killed Clare. Why?'

I kept asking him why. Why did he do it? Why didn't he come and talk to me? I would have been able to sort it out. He said it was not like that, it just happened. He could not remember any of it. He still had no proper clothes, only those paper things they had given him. My dad was in a mess, seeing his son like that in a prison cell and being escorted down the stairs. It was just awful. Then we did not see him till the following week.

We saw Peter every week at the Magistrates' Court when he was remanded in custody. We could not visit him before or afterwards, but the whole family turned up every Thursday at nine to be in court for him. We would get rid of the kids and make sure we were there – my mum, my dad, my brother and my sisters. We felt we had to make that effort because he needed our support. We wanted him to see us there and know we were behind him all the way. We were the only people there every week. It was worse than awful: I felt so helpless to see my brother in the dock, with me able to do nothing. I just wanted to grab him and hold him. I wanted to hug him and say: 'Look, I'm here.' I did not want him up there by himself. That was the worst bit. The first time my mum stood up in court and started crying because she wanted to hold Peter. The magistrate told her to sit down and behave.

The whole family was badly affected by it. My mum went to pieces over what had happened. She would not talk about it or cry. My brother Tom, who is younger than Peter, would not talk about what had happened either. All he would say was 'I'll do this and I'll do that. I'll help with money and I'll drive here and there.' He would not talk at all about what he was feeling. Julie felt bad because she was in Wales and could not be with the family. She wanted to come over and stay here, but she had two children to look after. Susan is the youngest, the baby of the family, and she could not stop crying. We all felt guilty and blamed ourselves. The night it happened we sat at my house and we all thought that if we had done something different or said something it might never have happened. I kept saying: 'It's my fault. He came to talk to me and I didn't have time. He came to me for help and I couldn't help him.'

Tom had seen Peter the night it happened. Peter had rung him and said: 'I need to talk to you. Come down the pub for a drink.' Tom had said he couldn't, but he would buy Peter a quick half, which he did, and then he left. So he blamed himself too, because, he said, if he had stayed, it would not have happened. My mum always said that she should have been here that night and it was her fault for going away. So we all blamed ourselves. At this time we did not blame Peter. With me that guilt lasted for months. I really felt that I could have done more. Looking back on it all now, I know that it might have happened even if we had talked, and if it had not happened that night, it might have happened at another time.

When I was at Peter's house after the killing, I had asked a policeman if I could take Andrew home from the hospital to look after him, because he had only been taken in to see if he was all right and I knew Peter would never harm him. The policeman said he would telephone me that night to go and pick him up, but the phone call never came. When I rang to find out what was happening. I was told that he had been taken to Clare's parents.

153

I rang them the next day, but they didn't want to talk to me. I don't blame them for that, but Andrew was still my nephew. They said we could not have any contact with Andrew at all if we were going to stay in touch with Peter. They wanted him to forget his dad.

We left it for a while to give them a bit of time. Peter had turned up and was being remanded in custody every week and we were busy dealing with that. Then it was Clare's funeral. I thought it best to keep away because our presence would only upset her parents even more. Two weeks later I phoned them again to ask if I could see Andrew. They refused. I wrote to Peter's lawyer, to ask if any of us, especially my mum, who was his grandma, could see Andrew. Peter's lawyer went round to their house to ask if I or my mum could see Andrew and they still said no. He got in touch with the social services, who went to Clare's parents' house and said they were too old to bring up Andrew because they were over sixty.

They were very bitter and never mentioned Peter's name to Andrew, which I could understand up to a point, but Peter was still his dad.

The social services came to see me and said that Clare's parents did not want visiting rights or to share him. I either had to have him or not. It was all or nothing. I said: 'Just bring him.' At this time Andrew was in playschool. Clare's father came to my house with a black bin-liner full of his toys and told me to pick him up at three o'clock from playschool. They had not told him that he was coming to me.

I picked him up and brought him home and told him that he was now going to live with me. We phoned Clare's parents a few times, because Andrew wanted to stay in touch with them. They would ask if he was still seeing Peter and when I said yes, they said that they did not want any more contact. They said that they could not understand why I was seeing my brother after what he had done to Clare or why I was keeping Andrew in touch with his dad. They said that if my family was going to keep in touch with Peter, they did not want anything to do with any of us. I have not heard from them since. Clare's daughter by her first marriage, Dawn, who is 21, hated Peter from the start. In fact quite a few of the arguments between Clare and Peter were caused by Dawn. However, she came to see Andrew a few times at our house, but then she stopped and for the past eighteen months we have had no contact at all with Clare's side of the family.

Clare's death was in March and the trial was on 28 November in Preston. It was the third trial date – they cancelled the first two. One was cancelled because the judge wanted to go home early for the weekend.

We wanted the whole family to be there for Peter but it was impossible. Susan and I were both due to be called as witnesses and neither of us could go in. We had to wait outside the whole time, which was awful. I was going to be the very last witness. I had wanted to talk about how Peter had completely changed in the year before the killing, becoming so depressed that he depended on anti-depressants and losing so much weight that he became scrawny and ill-looking. In the end they did not call me because Peter's lawyer felt that provocation had been proved.

Mum did not go at all because she could not bear it. She was so badly affected by it that she went into a shell and would not talk to anyone about it. We all knew she was trying to be strong but it was not working. She just tried to shut the trial out of her mind. She did not even want to know the date. My dad was there every day.

The people in the family who could go to the trial were dotted around the court so that wherever Peter looked he could see one of us and he knew we were there for him. During the trial Clare's family sat behind Peter, so that when he walked in and out of court they were the first people he would see. They did it on purpose. The police sat by the side and they used to talk to Clare's parents. It was awful for Peter.

When we had to wait in the waiting room and her parents were there, they made a point of staring at us all the time and if looks could kill I would not be here now. If we went to the toilet they would come in and make comments about Peter being a murderer, and as the murderer's family, we were all the same. This made the trial hard. It was Peter who had done it, not me or the rest of my family.

The day the verdict was due, I went into the court room early and bagged all the places behind Peter for our family, which meant Clare's parents could not sit there and that when the verdict came through, he would see us first, before anybody else. It was important to me that Peter knew his family were there. When the trial finished, we were told there would be a wait of an hour or two before the verdict came in. Peter asked someone to tell me to go and get some dinner for him. When I came back, my sister, my brother and my dad were outside the court waiting for me, because the jury had come back really quickly, within 25 minutes. Their verdict was not guilty of murder, but guilty of manslaughter. He got three years. I was crying and screaming in the street because I was so relieved. I knew he was not guilty of murder and they had proved it. I was crying, Susan was crying, my dad was crying; Tom was not. We went to see Peter in court, but we still couldn't touch him. I just wanted to hold him and hug him but I was not allowed to. Then he got taken to prison and we went off to phone my mum and tell her.

Clare's family might have felt we were all guilty, but not our friends in Glasgow. My mum lived round the corner from Peter and Clare, and she got a lot of support from that street to help her through it. We had lived there for 30 years, and my brothers, sisters and I had virtually been born there, and the whole street was behind us because they knew what Peter was like. He was never a bad lad, never had any trouble at school, and he was always well behaved. The neighbours brought flowers, a fruit bowl and a lot of things, just to show they cared. Peter got a lot of sympathy and he had many letters from people he knew in Glasgow, saying they could not understand why he had done it but they would stand by him because they knew what he was like.

I lost my job at the clothes shop because of the amount of time I had to take off work to deal with Andrew. I went back to the place where I had worked with my sister for nine years and they were really wonderful. A lot of people said how sorry they were and that it could have happened to anybody, and said that if I wanted anything just to ask. I had a few people ringing up and calling me a murderer, but it did not bother me.

The press, however, were completely against Peter. They just went on about man killing wife. They turned up at my mum's house one day, but she told them to bugger off. The only decent thing they said, which came out at the trial, was that Peter sent Clare a rose every day. The court coverage was all one-sided, and the defence did not appear in the papers at all. When he was given three years they printed the outrage from Clare's side of the family. I could understand that, because I would have felt the same. They printed interviews with Clare's neighbours which were lies, but they never tried to come and see me. The only mention of me was when Andrew came to live with me and then the headline was: KILLER'S SISTER TAKES IN SON WHO SAW MURDER.

About six months later I felt terribly depressed and just cracked up. I could not talk and I could not stop crying. All I could think about was my brother in jail for killing Clare. I also hated the thought of Clare in a grave. At the trial there were pictures of Clare naked, showing the stab wounds, which I had seen before the trial. It made me feel helpless that Clare was dead and Peter was by himself in prison and I could not do anything for either of them. I wanted to take Peter home and look after him, and bring Clare back.

I was clear about one thing: that my brother was not a murderer. I knew he did not do it on purpose and he did not plan it. Somebody said to me: 'You do know that Peter murdered Clare, don't you?'

I said: 'No, he didn't, he killed her.'

He did not do it deliberately, and that is what a murderer is, someone who deliberately does it. If I thought he had gone out and planned it I might feel differently about it. The whole family agree with that. I have known Peter for 30 years and I could not suddenly stop loving him because of this, even though it is wrong and it is awful.

If I had ever hoped to forget what Peter had done, dealing with Andrew was a constant reminder. Andrew came to me in the May, two months after it had happened and just before his fourth birthday. Peter asked if he could see Andrew and Andrew said he wanted to see his dad. I took him to see Peter, but he didn't like the prison at all. Clare's daughter, Dawn, said that if I was not careful, she would take Andrew away from me, so I applied to be Andrew's guardian. I didn't want Andrew to get settled with us and then be taken away. The social services and my lawyer encouraged me all the way and the court agreed to it.

Andrew was an absolute nightmare at the beginning. The first five months were hell. He had to have someone sleeping with him all night, every night. Mostly it was me, but Martin and Emily also took turns at it. No one ever got a night's sleep with him because he used to wake up screaming, kicking his arms and legs. He also used to wet the bed.

As Clare's parents had told him that his daddy had killed his mum and gone away, he thought he had lost his daddy as well and that they were both dead. When I told him that his dad was alive and in prison, he said: 'No. He's dead. He's gone.'

Andrew would not talk to anybody. He used to mumble loudly and it was quite frightening. I had lost my job by then and I spent the whole day with him. He used to follow me round the house while I did the housework and then he would sit on my knee and we would cuddle and talk for hours. Whatever he wanted to know I would tell him. I never lied to him, but I tried to explain to him what happened that night without going into too many gory details.

Four months later he was still wetting the bed and he kept saying this horrible word, which I could not make out. I went to Peter's solicitor and said that I wanted to know exactly what Andrew had seen that night, because until I did, I felt that I couldn't help him. He showed me the pictures of Clare when she was found, because I thought that if I could actually see through Andrew's eyes what he saw and could visualise the last picture in his mind of his mother I might be able to understand him. In the pictures Clare looked as if she were asleep, but her mouth was full of blood. When Andrew was screaming and shaking, he would shout 'bleah, bleah'. After I saw the pictures I thought that he was choking, like his mum when he saw her, with blood in his mouth. Two nights later when he started screaming and going 'bleah, bleah', I said 'It's blood.'

He looked at me and said: 'How do you know it's blood?'

I told him that I had seen pictures of his mummy and that I knew what he had seen.

He said: 'She had blood in her mouth and I tried to wash it off.'

He had not told anyone else, but once he knew that I had seen his mummy with blood in her mouth, he talked to me more about it. It was not miraculous, but he seemed to start sleeping easier and talked to me more. He told me that he had tried to wash his mum's face because he had wanted her to wake up – he thought she was asleep. I told him that she was not asleep, and she had gone to heaven by that time. I think it helped him knowing that somebody else knew what he had seen.

About a month later things had improved but he still kept wetting the bed. I feel that if a child is wetting the bed he has a deep-rooted problem. I wrote to Dora Black, a psychologist at the Royal Free Hospital in London who specialises in dealing with children like Andrew, who have seen their parents die violently or being murdered. I was finding him difficult to deal with because he was really nasty and naughty to Emily, and I felt as if I still wasn't getting anywhere. I don't believe in smacking children, but

I came close to it with Andrew at that time. I went to see Dora Black and she told me that what I had done so far was good. I felt good because she was the first person who had told me that I was doing something right. I had just been plodding along with Andrew, and I had never seen a child like it. She said the nastiness was part of the process, and he would get through it, which he did. He's fine now, his school work is brilliant and he is very close to his dad. He still talks about it sometimes, but nothing like as much as he used to.

When Peter came out of prison, after fourteen months, he came to stay with me. The probation people said that he could not go to my mum, because her house was on the same estate where he had been living with Clare, and he had nowhere else to go. He came to me for a couple of weeks but it did not work out because Andrew got to the stage where it was his dad against me. By the time Peter came out, we were into a routine and Andrew was part of our family. I was his mum, Martin was Martin and Emily was his sister. He was settled. We had not known Peter was coming out until the night before, when I had a phone call telling me to meet him at the train station. Even Peter didn't know he was coming out until then and he had asked someone to ring me. He had had a release date a couple of weeks before, but somehow the press got hold of it and told Clare's parents that he was coming out and asked how they felt about it. There was uproar – I've kept all the press cuttings. The Home Office denied it and when he actually came out it was kept quiet.

Peter was finding it hard to come to terms with being outside. I also found it very difficult having him living with us. I had Martin, Emily and Andrew to look after, but when Peter was there I felt I had to sit and talk to him. I felt I could not be a housewife to Martin, Emily and Andrew as well as a sister to Peter: I was torn. Peter moved out into a flat, and even though he was always at our house, it was easier than when he lived with us all the time. We tried to be normal but we couldn't because Peter needed to talk all the time about what he had done; he still hasn't got over what he did, and he always feels guilty. He blames himself all the time. He could not think about having another girlfriend. I just want to shake him and tell him that to a certain degree he has paid for it. He has done his time and the courts think it is right for him to come out. It is time to start living, but he cannot. We have our lives to carry on and we can't keep going over the past.

When he first came out, he was a mess. He was always crying and talking about it all the time. I didn't want Andrew and Emily being reminded of it too much but he just went on about how guilty he felt, he could not drop it. He was only in there for fourteen months and I think he should have served his three years, because he was not ready to come out. When he was inside he was getting help, talking to people and he was being punished for what he had done, which was what he needed. He had psychiatrists, psychologists and probation officers all helping him. I cannot fault the way he was treated. One day he was in prison because he had killed his wife, the next he was out living with a normal family, trying to live a normal day-to-day life. He couldn't do it, it was just too quick for him and for all of us.

We still have Andrew living with us, but not all the time because he spends a lot of time with his dad. He goes there for most of the holidays because I am working again, which is better for me because I have had some help for the first time in ages. At one time I was doing everything – looking after Andrew, Emily and Martin as well as visiting Peter, taking Andrew down with me. Peter does not work. He has tried to get work but once they find out what he has done they aren't interested. He has a one-bedroom flat now, so Andy can sleep there, and the family are helping to furnish it slowly by giving him furniture from our houses.

It has totally changed my life, not just emotionally but materially as well. I lost a good job which was worth a lot of money, and the only work I can get now is part-time.

We had plans and had booked holidays which had to be cancelled, because one minute there were two good wages and the next just Martin's. We had no financial help with Andrew, I had to give money to Peter every month and my mum got into debt so I had to pay out for her as well. On top of that we had this three-year-old boy who disrupted our lives for a year. It is getting better now, a lot better, but it has totally changed my life.

Emotionally it has taken a lot out of me. When it first happened, apart from feeling that I had to do something, it did not hit me. Now I think a lot of Clare. She is the first person I have known who has died and I hate the thought of her being buried. When I am ironing or washing Andrew's clothes or putting him to bed I think, it shouldn't be me doing this, it should be his mum. Andrew should be being looked after by his mum – it is not fair on Clare, it is not fair on Andrew. I feel guilty that I am replacing her. I blame Peter for depriving Andrew of his mother. I don't hate him, but I blame him. I just wish he had got out of the house, out of the situation, instead of killing her. Even so, I think it would have happened anyway. I believe in fate.

When it first happened I was being strong and organising things. About six months later I couldn't stop crying and I couldn't cope with life. I didn't want to see anybody and I didn't want to talk to anybody. I used to unplug the telephone so that I did not have to talk to anyone. I would take Emily to her school, Andrew to his, and then I would come back home and do nothing. My house was a mess and I like my house. That was when I went to a counsellor, Shirl, who specialised in dealing with people who had relatives in prison. My sister, Julie, had seen an article about her and met her. Julie wanted me to see her as well, but I don't like going to people for help. I just wanted to sort it out by myself. At that time I did not share things. But my brother-in-law took me to see Shirl, who put her arms round me and I told her everything. I told her how guilty I felt for not having enough time for Peter that day. She

162

asked me if I was so important that I could have stopped it. She made me feel a lot better, that I could not have changed it. It was going to happen. I think Clare knew that, too, from some of the things she wrote in her diary, and from the way she egged Peter on and forced him to do things. She wanted something to happen, but she didn't think he would go that far.

Of course I shall never be able to forget it. I have Andrew, and it is always there. I remember Clare's birthday every year and I always put a piece in the paper, in memoriam.

Susan

Four years ago Susan's father was found guilty of murdering her mother. From the day he was charged, Susan was the only member of her family to stand by him. He pleaded not guilty and still denies killing his wife. Susan now lives in a council house on the outskirts of Birmingham with her husband and two children, who are both at secondary school. Her husband, Dave, has a degenerative bone disease which has turned a man who was a windsurfing instructor a year ago into a housebound invalid. He has difficulty walking anywhere and spends most of his days watching sport on television. There is a poster in their house showing a windsurfer on the ultimate wave in Hawaii as a constant reminder of what life used to be like. Susan works part-time in a chemist's shop just round the corner from where she lives, which allows her to return home easily if her husband needs her. She thinks she will have to give up the job in the next year as Dave's disease gets progressively worse because he will need constant care. She and Dave are in their mid-thirties and have been happily married for eighteen years.

She has chosen to remain anonymous because she is terrified of reprisals from her family, who believe she should not be giving any support to her father and have threatened her and her own family. The interview took a few hours because she found telling me all about it so upsetting that she would break down in tears. We would then take a break while she recovered and talk about our families and children. There were no barriers put up. I sent the story back to her to make sure she felt happy about it and she rang me to say that she was stunned by it, because she hadn't realised that was what she thought. I was only the third person she had talked to about it and she felt she had opened up too much. However, she decided that only the names needed changing.

I always thought of my family as just ordinary. There were five of us, three boys and two girls, and I was the eldest. My mother stayed at home to look after us until I was about seven and then she got a job as a home help. She progressed to become a warden at a sheltered unit.

We lived in Birmingham and my father worked at the airport. He left there to start his own business, doing welding and anything else with metals. He worked very hard. He was a very loving man and always supported the family, making sure we had everything he could afford, in particular a holiday every year. He was also a very strict man.

I left home when I was eighteen to get married. I couldn't wait to get out, because I didn't get on very well with my mum. I was just an ordinary teenager having rows with my mum. When we were married my husband, Dave, and I moved to Newquay because his family owned a hotel down there. We bought our own house and worked in the hotel which meant I did not see very much of my parents.

When Dave was made redundant after eleven years, we decided to give up everything and travel abroad for a few years with our two children. We had already arranged for my parents to come to us for Christmas, so they decided to come out and see us in Israel where we were spending it. We were really happy that my parents had come out to see us, particularly my mum, because she and my husband had a real love-hate relationship. My parents had been against me marrying Dave and refused to go to my wedding. As time went on, they slowly accepted him, but it took four or five years for my mother to speak to him. In Israel they got on really well. Dave used to joke with my mum, saying, 'I travel three thousand miles and you still come and get me for Christmas.' They used to call each other names but they would laugh about it and it was playful.

My parents stayed with us for a week and we really had a good time. My mother and I sorted out our problems because we had some time on our own, and we talked things through. Mum finally realised that, after twelve years, I was serious about Dave and that he did make me happy. I think she had been frightened that he would hurt me, but now she realised he would not. For the first time she actually cried in front of me: when they left, she said that she wished that she did not have to go. The one thing I really wanted her to tell me was that she loved me, because all my life she had never told me that. Not once. But she didn't. Since then I have found out a lot more about my mother's life and the kind of person she was. I don't think she was capable of loving anybody, because her childhood was so awful. I don't think she ever got any love, except from my father, who really loved her.

That was the last time I saw her.

A few weeks after my parents had left, there was a battle between the Israelis and the Arabs near where we were sleeping in our van, and there were guns firing right over the top of it. We decided that it was no longer safe for the children and that we should return to Europe. Originally we had been planning to go on travelling east – and if it had been only Dave and I we would have stayed in Israel for a while because it was such a beautiful country – but we decided that we could not take risks with young children.

We made our way to a fishing village on a Greek island where no one spoke English and we had to learn Greek just to get by. It was lovely, and my parents said that they would come and see us in the summer and spend a holiday with us, but sadly that never happened.

In spite of all the travelling, I made sure that I stayed in touch with both sets of parents wherever we went, by giving them the address of a post office or somewhere, and we wrote to each other at least once a fortnight. In March I did not hear from my mother for about thre weeks and I had a feeling that something was wrong. I telephoned her and had terrible problems getting through, because the phone kept going dead. When I did get hold of her, she said that everything was fine and there was nothing wrong with her or my father. I had this feeling that something was wrong but she kept saying that she and my father were fine.

Every time I telephoned my mother, I would tell her that I loved her, but that time when the phone went dead I did not have time to tell her. A few days later it was Mothers' Day, but I forgot all about it and didn't send her a card. The next week she was dead.

I found out when I got a telegram from my sister to ring home. I was ill that day with food poisoning, so Dave phoned my sister, who told him that my mother was dead. She had been murdered. My sister told Dave that my father had killed my mother, but Dave did not pass that on. He just said that someone had killed her. We decided not to tell the children the whole story; instead we just told them nanny had been killed in a road accident.

When Dave told me my mum was dead, my immediate reaction was: 'Oh God. How is Daddy?' My first thought was for my father, wondering how he would be able to cope without my mother.

We had some very nice Greek friends who took the children off our hands and looked after them while we tried to make arrangements to get back to England. Our friends said that they would look after them until we came back but the authorities would not allow it because they were worried that we might not come back and that the children would then become the responsibility of the government. It was too expensive for us all to fly back. In any case, we discovered that we couldn't do that because we were not allowed to leave our van in Greece. It had a lot of wind-surfing gear – Dave was a windsurfing instructor – and when we left we had to take it because it had been checked through Greek customs with us. Sorting out the red tape had already taken two weeks and I was desperate to get back to see my father. It would have taken far too long to drive back so instead we decided that I would go home on my own leaving Dave in Greece with the children. The only thing that was in my mind was getting home to see my dad because he means the world to me.

My father was living with my middle brother and they both came to meet me at the airport to take me back to my brother's house. When we got into the car, they told me that my father had been accused of killing my mother. I was completely devastated, because it was the first time I had heard anything about this. I wondered how anybody could think that my father could do such a thing. I was shown the news clippings about my mother: there was an awful lot of detail in the local papers. I was very upset by them.

My dad went to his room and my brother told me that things had not been brilliant between my mum and dad just before the killing. She had been seeing another man and had decided that although she and Dad would go on living together, she would stop sleeping with him. My parents had a flat in the sheltered housing unit where my mother worked because she was on twenty-four-hour duty. She also had a separate office, with its own front door, which had a bed, a toilet and a sink, where the duty warden slept on the one day my mother was allowed off. She told my father that she would sleep in there and he could have the bedroom in the flat.

Her first night in the office was a Saturday and she was murdered on the Sunday morning. She was killed in the office. When I got there the flat was still locked up because the police wanted to check it out. Dad was staying at my brother's because he had nowhere else to go.

Just before her death, Mum had spent a week with my sister. Everybody in the family knew that she was having an affair, except me, of course – they did not tell me as they felt I was living too far away. I didn't think my mother would ever do anything like that. While she was staying at my sister's, this man had come to meet her and they had slept in my sister's bed. How anybody could do that I do not know.

My father stayed in to look after my brother's three young children, all under four, while I went for a walk with my brother. There was a big field by the house and we just walked round and round it. My brother said to me: 'Susan, I had a row on Sunday morning with Mother. I told her: "The best thing that could happen to you is for someone to come and kill you because you are a whore. You have put this family through hell." That was the last thing I said to her and now she is dead. She broke Dad. He was a broken man.'

I had flown into Heathrow on the Friday and we spent the weekend talking. I found out that my father had been questioned by the police and spent three days in the police station, but they did not have enough evidence and had to let him go. My father had to let the police know where he was going and check in with them every now and again, but he had not been charged.

My aunt came round to my brother's house and the whole family was there apart from my sister and my eldest brother, Mark. My sister did not want anything to do with my father because she was convinced that he had killed my mother. The rest of us thought that he could never do a thing like that. Mark was confused and almost thought that if he didn't see my father then my mother hadn't died and it might all just be a bad dream. None of us found it easy to come to terms with it, but he was particularly affected.

My mother had died in a most horrific way. Mark was with my father when they found her and afterwards he had just gone into hiding. His ex-girlfriend was the only person who knew where he was.

The whole family had fallen apart and, being the eldest, I felt I had to be strong for everybody and keep them going. My mum used to do that, and I felt that was what mums should do. Of course we were no longer children – I was 31 at the time and the youngest was 23 – but we were all devastated. It was a very stressful time for everybody and we tried to help each other. My main concern was for Dad, who was the person I felt needed the most help. He had started drinking and smoking heavily.

We spent a terrible weekend together and I never want to spend one like that again. Anyone who has gone through a murder will know what I am talking about – you can only know what it is like if you have been through it. You feel as if your whole world has fallen apart, as if you are in a big, black tunnel and there is no light anywhere. You feel as if you are going down and down and you will never reach the bottom. It is the most awful feeling and it never leaves you.

My grandparents, my mother's parents, were paralysed by the news. How can you explain to somebody that their child is dead? You do not ever expect to bury your child. They were very old, in their seventies and eighties. My grandfather had been blinded during the war and did not go out much. He relied on my nan and my mum to do things for him. He and my nan lived just down the road from my mum, so they saw her at least once a week. My grandfather idolised her, and me, because when his other children had their kids no one would let him hold them as they thought he would drop them. I was the first grandchild he had ever held. My mother did not stop him because, although he was blind, he could sense things a lot better than sighted people, and we had a very special relationship. He took her death very hard. He would not drink or eat. He just could not cope with the fact that his daughter had gone.

On the Monday after I arrived, the police phoned to tell us that my mother's flat had been released although the office was still closed. My father and brother went to the flat to get the keys. My father decided he could not bear to live there again but we did have to sort out the flat. I knew my father could not cope with it on his own. None of my brothers or sisters wanted to touch my mother's things. My brother even refused to have anything of my mother's in the house or to go into the flat. It was left for me to sort out, but I still had my family in Greece and I could not spend months in England. I had never left my children before and my husband had never been left to look after the kids on his own. Obviously, I was thinking of them constantly. Yet they were not of as much concern to me as my father, even though I was thinking about them a lot.

On the Tuesday we went to the flat. I asked my dad what he wanted to do with the clothes and he decided that as no one wanted them, we would give them to a charity shop. My mother was very fussy about clothes. She had to have new things every week and her bedroom was jam-packed with clothes and underwear. She had 50 or 60 skirts alone. She must have had 30 or 40 pairs of shoes in every colour and shade you could imagine, with a handbag to match every pair. Everything always had to be matching: if she wore a certain shade of green, everything had to be in that shade, right down to her underwear. She would not be seen in the same clothes two days running; in fact if she went out in the morning and then again in the afternoon, she would change in between.

My father would not come into the bedroom, and it was left to me to deal with all the clothes. It took me three or four days to pack everything up. Case after case. It seemed never-ending. Father kept wandering around.

On Thursday or Friday, we were in the flat and there was a knock on the door. Someone from the council had come to say that they could now release the office and they wanted it cleared of mother's things as soon as possible so that they could move someone else in there. My father got himself into a terrible state about going into the office and I realised I could not let him do it. I told him I would clear it out. He tried to stop me but I reassured him that I was fine and could easily do it.

I expected to go in and find the place normal, but when

I went into the office I found that the police had not cleared anything up. There was blood, my mother's blood, everywhere: all up the walls, on the carpet, on the bed, all over the wardrobe and the furniture. I was thankful I had not let my dad see it. I had had no idea that it would have been left in such a state; they had not cleaned anything. I had to touch my mother's blood to get her things out.

I will never get over seeing that room. It is a picture in my mind which will never, ever leave me. It is very hard to explain what that does to a person: to go into a room and see that and to know it is your mother's blood is the most horrific thing that can ever happen. I was on the verge of being hysterical. I knew I had to keep my screaming and crying very low-key as otherwise my father, who was sitting just outside the door, would come running in. I desperately did not want him to see it. I have to live with it for the rest of my life. I think that the police and the council were very wrong to let me and my family see that. I know someone has got to see it, but surely there are people who are trained to do these things. Surely it would not hurt somebody who is not involved as much as the person's daughter to see that. I just got hold of everything as quickly as I could and got out of there.

I had been told only that my mother had been murdered. Even though we had talked about it, nobody had said how. I had always been Daddy's girl and my father had protected me from everything since I was a tiny child. I was lucky enough to find a husband who was exactly the same and I had been sheltered from a lot all my life. In those few moments I grew up so fast. Seeing all that blood, I realised that I was not a little girl any more.

I suppose that until I had seen that blood, I had tried to think that it was all right: my mum had just gone away. I felt that it was not really my mum we were talking about; it was somebody completely different and my mum was going to be fine. After seeing that room, I knew she was not fine, that she was really dead. She was gone and all I could think was that I had forgotten Mothers' Day.

I desperately wanted to hear her voice, because I had seen so little of my mother over the previous twelve years and most of our contact had been on the telephone. Her voice meant more to me than anything.

When I came out of the room, my father saw that I was not in the best of states. I must have been very white and shaking because my father just took one look at me and said, 'Oh, my God.'

We took everything upstairs to the flat and went straight to my nan's house. They plied me with whisky because I had had such a shock. To this day I have never told anybody in the family, except Dave, what that room was like. I didn't think that anybody else could take it. It is something that I know I will have to live with, but no one else should. I know what it is doing to me and I don't think that the rest of the family should have to live with that. It is bad enough for us that Mum is dead.

My father was not coping very well. He never said who he thought had killed Mum. He just said that he thought that someone had come in and killed her, because he was asleep upstairs and Mother was downstairs in the office. I believed him because I could never have thought that it was my father. I knew he was strict, and I had been told that a few weeks before he had hit Mother and given her a black eye. They had had a row and he had hit her. I still never thought he could actually have killed her. We knew that her murderer must have been somebody she knew because she had opened the door in her nightie. The police thought that there had been a knock on the door and she had opened it, turned around and walked back into the office. Then the murderer hit her from behind. She knew so many people, as she was the warden, that it could have been one of any number of people, even a relative of someone in the unit.

My father was very upset: he was just in a daze, acting like a zombie. He was drinking a lot, about a bottle of whisky a day, and smoking all the time. He cried a lot and he was totally devastated. It is impossible to say that an

174

innocent man would react in one way and a guilty man in another. I was in such a state of shock, and so aware of my own pain, that although I was obviously aware of his, it did not register much. I just remember him drinking so much and wanting to talk about Mother all the time.

He kept saying how much he loved her and telling me that the police were making up the story about the man she was seeing. He said that there was no way she would do something like that to him. At other times he seemed confused. He told me that the first 25 years they were together were the happiest years of her life, but after their 25th wedding anniversary she had told him that she did not feel so in love with him. He told me stories about what had happened at the beginning of their life together and he would put Mum down. He had never been like that before, and I think that he was in a state of confusion. Still I did not believe he could have done anything like that to her, or even harm her, because he truly loved her.

He had had a terrible childhood. He was beaten by his parents and was basically left to bring himself up. Neither of them had good childhoods. The only person who ever showed him any love, apart from my mother, was one of his sisters; his mother never did. My father's childhood was poverty-stricken. His family did not have two pennies to rub together, and when my parents met, the council flat my father lived in still did not have electricity. My mum's family lived in a private house and she had everything, a cushy life compared to Dad's, but the one thing she could never get was love. Everything else, material-wise, she had. They made a good match because they propped each other up: they clung on to each other because each was loved by the other one. That was the missing link they both found. Knowing what I do now about my parents, I feel they were frightened that if either of them let the other go nobody else would love them. They were prepared to put up with anything just as long as they had each other.

I think that if Dad had left her when things did start going wrong, Mum would be alive today. But they had been married for 29 years and they were frightened of losing that.

I wanted to go back to Greece and see my children again, but first I decided I had to see my eldest brother, who had gone to ground. I wanted to feel that I had left the country with as much sorted out as possible. I got in touch with his ex-girlfriend and arranged to meet him. Mark insisted that we met in a pub and that I came alone. He told me the story of how he found my mum. He had been staying with my parents after breaking up with his girlfriend. My mother had not wanted anybody to know that she was not sleeping in the flat with my father, because she was very much into putting on a nice front. She wanted people to think that everything was just perfect. So she wanted to come back up to the flat by half past six in the morning so that nobody in the unit would know that she was sleeping downstairs in the office.

When she had not come up by that time, Dad went down and knocked on the door and called out to her. She did not answer and the curtains were still drawn, which he thought was a bit funny, but not wanting to upset her he went back upstairs to the flat for about ten or fifteen minutes. Then he went back down and called her again. There was no answer. He kept ringing the doorbell to the office, but still there was no reply. He went up to get Mark, who was in bed. Dad woke him up and said, 'I can't get any reply from Mum. Do you think we should break down the door, just in case she is hurt inside, or do you think we should get the police?'

I don't know why he said the police. Why would he want to get the police?

They decided to break the door down. Dad got the crowbar out of the back of his car and they opened the door. Just inside they found Mum lying there, dead. Mark pushed Dad out of the way and told him to get out, but Dad went into the bathroom to be sick. You would do, wouldn't you, if your wife was lying there with hardly any head? Then he thought that he needed a cigarette to stop him being ill. He knew Mum smoked and walked back into that room and stepped over my mother to get a packet of cigarettes. I don't understand that, I really don't, but who can tell what people do in such a state of shock? That is how my father explained his bloody footprints being there. Maybe it was true – I wasn't there so I wouldn't know. Then they called the police.

My mother had been dead three days before I was sent a telegram.

By the time I went back to Greece they still hadn't charged my father.

My mother used to leave cash lying around all over the place. She had piles of coins everywhere – in the kitchen, the dining room, the office, her bedroom, and in her bags. However, when I sorted out Mum's stuff, I never found a penny. I thought that was very strange, as the police had said it was not a burglary.

My mum also always wore jewellery, not just one piece but often six or seven pieces at the same time, including necklaces, rings and bracelets, charm bracelets and earrings. She had a thing about jewellery. Yet none of that was found, either. I went to the police station the day after I had gone into the office. I had never been in a police station in my life before. The man who saw me was scum. When I went into that room, a woman whose mother was dead, who had just been to the place where her mother was murdered and seen all her blood, all he said was: 'Yeah, what do you want?'

I tried to explain to him that there was no money or jewellery. All he said to me was: 'We've got him. We've got him. Your dad, we've got him.'

He just could not care less. I couldn't understand why he should be like that to somebody like me, because at the time they had not charged Dad or anything. He just kept saying to me: 'We've got him sussed. We've got him. He's the one we're after.' I was crying. I said: 'How can you say that it wasn't a burglary when you haven't got the jewellery?'

'We do have some jewellery,' he said.

'Let me see it.'

'No.'

'How do I know if it is my mother's or not if you won't let me see it?'

'You have not seen her for a long time, so how would you know?' he replied.

I told him that my mother had had jewellery for years and years and I would recognise it. He just bundled me out of his room, still saying, 'We've got him.'

I went back to Greece and they finally released my mother's body to be buried three months after her murder. I did not go to the funeral because nobody told me about it. My middle brother told the family he had contacted me, but he didn't. Nobody believed me and I was in the family's bad books, because I had not even sent flowers. My grandfather had a neck brace, after having a fall, and the hospital had told him he must never take it off. The moment he got home from the funeral he took it off and within three days he was dead. Once he had buried Mum he just did not see any reason to carry on living. He basically killed himself because he took off the brace. So there was another funeral, and again no one informed me about it.

My father had been charged with the murder about a month earlier, in May, but he did not go to jail. The police just put him on bail and he didn't even have to report to them, unless he was going out of the area. My brother chucked him out of the house and the whole family was against him. He went to live with a friend from work.

By that time we had left Greece and gone off again on our travels. As no date was set for the trial, we decided not to come home immediately. Looking back on it, I don't know whether it was the right or wrong thing to have done. At the time I thought I was doing right and I suppose I was frightened of the responsibility.

Things did not work out for my dad and he was put into a bail hostel, but I didn't know about this. Round about

Christmas, I just had to come home. There was just something in me which said: 'You have got to go home now.'

We came back to England with nowhere to live. We did not have very much money left. I phoned up my middle brother and he put us up. He told us that Dad was in a bail hostel. Dad spent Christmas walking around on his own because no one wanted him. I managed to find him. We were put into a bed and breakfast hotel because we had nowhere to live and I found Dad a room in a house, to get him out of the hostel. I looked after him, did his washing and his ironing, and cooked his meals. He had lost a lot of weight and although he was only 50 he looked about 70 years old. He spent most of his time with us. His business had folded and the only work he could get was working for somebody else.

He was finally given a date to go to court. By that time we had at last got a temporary council house. Dad still spent most of his time with us, even sleeping at our house.

Both Mum's brothers and mine were after Dad and wanted to get him. We were with him all the time. Even when he went to court, he was still on bail. Throughout the prosecution he was still coming home to us every night, which was amazing considering that it was a murder trial. The only time they took Dad into custody was when he started giving his evidence.

They still haven't found the weapon that killed my mother. Basically, whoever killed her hit her and just could not stop. It was a frenzied attack. She had quite a lot of injuries. Everybody in the family believed that Dad did it. I didn't.

My father was sentenced to life imprisonment. I went to the trial for only one day, and then only because I was a witness for the defence. I was the only one in the family who gave evidence for the defence. All the others were witnesses for the prosecution. It was the summer holidays and I had nobody to look after the children, so the only time I went was to give evidence. The rest of the time Dave went with him, every single day.

179

The trial lasted about a month. When the jury found Dad guilty, my middle brother went berserk trying to get him. He is a very violent person and has actually done time for beating up a policeman. The police knew what his reaction would be and were ready for him. It took nearly six policemen to hold him down and they had to put him in the cells downstairs.

Dave came back and had to tell me, although I knew as soon as I saw the car draw up without Dad in it. Then we had to tell the children.

When we came back to England, we had sat down with Dad and told the children the truth about Mum being murdered and Dad being accused of it. We decided to do this partly because I don't like to lie to people, but also because it was going to be in the local paper and I didn't want them to find out like that and think their parents had lied to them.

When Dave told me that Dad had got life, I tried to compose myself a little before we went in to tell the children. If I had been upset, I knew it would make them upset. I didn't know for nearly a week where my father had been sent. The whole of the family – my brothers, sisters, aunts, uncles and grandparents – didn't want anything to do with him. In fact I was frightened to leave the house because I had threats made against me. I would not even go to the garden to put the washing out, because I was so frightened, as I had stuck by my dad all this time.

I have since found out that my mother was pregnant with me before she married and that Dad might not even be my father. He swears he is, but how does he know? The only person who could have told me was my mother, and she can't now, can she? But he is the one who brought me up whether he is my father or not.

To this day I don't know whether he killed my mum or not. I was not there and until I am 100 per cent certain, I couldn't turn my back on him, and even then I don't think I could.

Even if he did admit he killed Mum I would go on seeing

180

him. I could never, ever not see him. To be honest, I would be relieved if he admitted it because then I would know that the right person is being punished and there is not somebody out there who is getting away with it. But, whoever killed my mother, whether it was him or someone else, I hope that he thinks about it, that he remembers every day of his life what he did to her and that he remembers every blow he gave her. I hope that, even if it is my father, because that is worse than any prison sentence he could be given – far, far worse.

I would say I am 80 per cent certain that he did it, but he still maintains, after doing four years in prison, that he didn't do it. Somebody who counselled me said that he has lost everything and he is too frightened of losing me if he admits it now. Until he admits it, he will never get out of prison, but it seems he would rather do 40 years than admit it.

It is very difficult for people to understand that even if somebody has killed another person whom you love, you can still love him. Of course you can never forgive him for what he has done, but you cannot stop loving him. Forgiving someone and loving someone are quite different. I may not like what someone has done – indeed I might be horrified by what he has done – but I still love him. He is still the same person. Everybody can get so angry that they are taken over the top and that is what I think happened with my Dad. He was just so angry thinking that she was sleeping with another man that he hit her and he could not stop. I truly believe that is what happened. Yet he is still the same man as he was before. He is a loving, awkward devil. He is Dad. Whether he spends ten, twenty or 30 years in prison, I don't think I could ever turn my back on him because he is my Dad.

I have put up with a lot from my family. They have all turned against me. They have even come back and harassed me and threatened me at work. When Dad does come out they will come back again, because they will want to know where he is. They want to kill him because of what he did to my mum. I have gone through a lot of hassle for him and I will for the rest of my life, and certainly until he is dead, but I cannot turn my back on him.

It is five years since my mother was murdered and my father has been in prison almost four years. I still have not got rid of the feeling of despair. When something like this happens your world falls apart. People say to me that time is a great healer and that as time goes on I will get over it. They don't know what they are talking about. You can never get over something like this. I am pulled in two ways, because not only am I the daughter of the victim, I am also the daughter of the murderer, which means my loyalties are divided.

My mother is dead and it is very hard to explain that although I love her there is nothing more I can do for her, but there is one parent who is still living and, whatever his reasons for doing something like this, I cannot give up on him. It is something which lives with me every day of my life. I have bad days and I have good days. As time goes by the better days come more and more but that does not mean that it ever leaves you.

Every day, I think about it. Just a little thing may spark it off. Somebody may walk along with their hair the same way as she wore hers and I think about it. I do not cry as much, nor do I look so ill, and I have started getting on with my life, but it is still all there. Before this happened I used to be a very outgoing person and had lots of friends, but now I don't trust anyone. I have been hurt so much that I don't have any friends because I will not allow people to get close. I have acquaintances to whom I say hello, but basically I keep myself to myself and as soon as anybody wants to get near, I shut them out. I have built a brick wall around myself and it gets higher and higher.

Since this happened, there has been only one person who has been able to knock a few of the bricks down, a counsellor to whom I have spoken a few times. But the bricks have gone back up again afterwards, because I am frightened of having anybody near me. I am so frightened of anybody finding out what happened.

People seem to shy away from you if your parent is known as a murderer. They think that there is something wrong with you as well. So I tend to be a very private person and I do not mention anything about it to anybody. If somebody asks me something about my mum and dad, such as are they alive or do I still see them, which is a normal subject of conversation, I say that my dad is alive. When asked where he lives, I tell them the area he is in jail. How long has he been living there? A few years. What does he do? Nothing much. I try to steer the conversation away from my parents as I don't like talking about them at all. I have had to let it be known to my family, my brothers, sisters, uncles and aunties, that I do not see my father any more, because if they knew, I would not be able to go out at all. I have even had to deny that.

Ruth

'Ruth' has chosen to remain anonymous to protect her family. Her son, Peter, had left his Glasgow home to live in London where he killed a young man with whom he was sharing a house. The murder led to his father, Tim, finally seeking help for his alcoholism which had plagued the family since the early days of his marriage. Ruth still goes to a self-help group for the families of alcoholics which has influenced the way she deals with her family and looks at her past life. She feels her son's crime was partly a consequence of the effect that alcohol had on the family. Like many people who have found an answer or help for a problem Ruth has adopted the philosophy of the self-help group for all her problems and uses the distinctive language of that particular group: she has to accept her life and accept other people's right to live theirs differently. The killing has become a terrible focus, with every incident in Peter's life seen as contributing to the murder.

Ruth is highly articulate in her broad Glasgow dialect, and as we sat in a hotel coffee shop she happily poured out her life story. She has had a hard life, with little money, and her husband's alcoholism has drained both her emotional strength and her finances. Now every day is spent thinking about Peter in prison, whom she feels is paying the price for the mistakes of herself and her husband.

She is a retired nurse, in her early sixties, and lives in Cumbernauld on the outskirts of Glasgow with her husband, who is crippled by a stroke. Peter is serving a life sentence in Weyland Prison, Norfolk. Her other two boys live in London.

185

I was the eldest child of a large, working-class, poor Catholic family – happy, but very poor and religious. I loved my family, but I had tensions about my loyalties because I wanted to be different. I went into nursing, and met Tim there. He had started as a nurse but became the hospital telephonist. He had a left-wing, almost communist, non-religious background. He was a bit of a rebel and trying to find himself.

We were both in our twenties and married six months after we met. We went to a residential adult further education college, called New Battle Abbey, because we had not stayed on at school and got Highers. It was a great experience. We were the only married couple, so they gave us a cottage to ourselves. After that, we both went back into nursing and decided to have a family. One problem was that Tim had started drinking. There was never any violence, but there was tension because I hated Tim when he'd had a drink. He was like two different people. I didn't know anything at all about alcoholism. The problem with having an alcoholic in the family is that it affects everyone. I think my reaction probably caused more harm than the drinking itself.

I became pregnant with Peter and it was a very difficult birth because I was such a long time in labour. In his infancy he was not a 'by-the-book' baby. I knew instinctively that something was wrong, almost from his first feed. I kept telling doctors and nurses this, but the medical people, while they were kind, said I was an anxious mother. We discovered he was pyloric, which means a muscle at the end of the stomach does not open and close normally. A very minor operation cures it, but I was so fanatical about doing everything right that I had obscured the symptoms, deciding that the medical people knew best. For instance, when he cried for a feed just after he had finished one, I thought he was still hungry. The clock shrank to just feeding Peter, there was nothing else. Finally, when the doctors discovered what was wrong with him, I was out of my head. I decided they were just saying it was an illness and really it was all my fault because I had not done the right thing. He had the wee operation and he was fine, but I was not. I just went to pieces and had a nervous breakdown. I was in hospital for about four weeks and had two doses of electro-convulsive therapy. I was fine after that.

When Douglas was born a year later, he was pyloric too, but I knew about it now and was able to tell the doctors. When Michael was born six years later I had a minor recurrence of the breakdown and had to go into hospital again.

During all this time there were ups and downs and tension in the family because of Tim's drinking, but there was nothing major. I was a terrible perfectionist, which was causing just as much trouble. If the boys came home with anything from school I would praise it, but then always find a fault. I always had to pick at things.

Tim and I would have heart-to-heart talks about his drinking and he would promise to stop, but I said that I didn't want him to give it up entirely, I just wanted him to have an occasional drink.

In 1970 Tim had a minor TB infection, caught from an old man in hospital, and had to leave nursing because he was no longer strong enough to lift people. He joined the civil service, and had to take a drop in wages because he began as just a clerical assistant. He had worked there for six years, taking the exams to become an executive officer, and was dealing with unemployed people with special needs when he had a stroke. He was 43.

I found his drinking even more difficult to deal with after that. I would either go out and spend unwisely or pretend that I was exaggerating his problem and that really he just liked a few drinks now and again.

The boys must have felt that they were not getting my attention, because I was obsessed with Tim, but I was very anxious for them. In spite of the problems between us I admired Tim a great deal. He taught himself to write with his left hand in his year off sick after the stroke, instead of just giving up. He went back to work for five years, but it was getting a bit too much for him and he decided to retire.

In 1982 Peter was 22, Douglas was 21 and Michael was fifteen. I was working part-time and Tim had his pension which meant we were OK. But then we had a fire. It was Peter's birthday and he had gone out drinking. We had gone to bed and some time later Peter had come home from a party. I was woken up by Michael's voice shouting: 'Peter! Peter!'

I got out of bed, went on to the landing and saw flames in the stairwell and Michael yelling down to the living room. I asked what he was doing. Michael said: 'Peter is down there. He is in the living room. I heard him coming in.'

Tim woke up and tried to go down the stairs in the flames. We pulled him back and got out of the window, jumping fifteen feet on to mattresses which we had thrown down. Michael immediately rushed off and called the fire brigade, who dragged Peter out and took him to hospital. He was suffering from smoke inhalation and was deeply unconscious, and he didn't come round for about 36 hours.

It turned out that Peter had come in and turned on the cooker to make himself a cup of coffee because the electric kettle was broken. The firemen thought he had turned on the wrong ring, because there was no saucepan on it, and gone back into the living room and fallen asleep while the flames took hold in the kitchen.

Peter was something of a gambler, but he was always a thoughtful, caring person where other people were concerned. He seemed driven at times by a need to make people happy. Just before Christmas one year he won about £300 and spent it all on presents for the family. I felt a wee bit uneasy about the gambling, but never for a moment understood that it was becoming a compulsion like his father's drink problem.

Peter joined the Socialist Workers' Party and was in the civil service, doing the same sort of job as his father had done. He was against the government and too young to realise that he could have his ideals and still be part of the system. He threw his job in, in spite of his managers trying to persuade him to stay, and went down to London, where his brother, Douglas, had been for about two years. There was nothing I could do about it. I used to feel through the years that in some way I should have been stricter, because I was hung up about respectability, but there was nothing really wrong with them.

Peter seemed to do fine in London after that. He was doing part-time jobs. When I visited, I didn't like the life-style down there, but that was their life and I just had to try to accept it. At home, Michael was still with us and he was fine. I was still reacting to Tim's drinking. I was trying to work out whether to leave him or not, because I was so weary of it by this time.

Peter stayed in touch. Tim and I went down to London for a week's holiday and stayed in a boarding house. I met Peter's girlfriend and we went to places like Regent's Park Zoo. I was not happy about his life because I was old-fashioned. My friends' and neighbours' sons and daughters were getting married and getting a house near their mum, and this is what I wanted for my own children. I now realise they have their own lives to lead in their own ways, and I do not want it now, but then I desperately wanted them to be like everybody else's children.

One night in April 1984 Douglas phoned me and said that Peter was in a bit of trouble and had been arrested. He said he would phone me back later and told me not to worry. In fact what he meant was that he was not going to tell me on the phone, because it was so serious. He had phoned my sister and she came over. I will always be able to picture the next few minutes, because it is the last clear memory I had for months: she stood in front of the fire-place and said: 'I've got a wee bit of bad news about Peter.' I knew then that just as our life seemed to be all right again something terrible was going to happen.

One of the boys who lived in Peter's house had been stabbed to death.

I said: 'Don't tell me. I just don't want to know,' as if I could get away with not being told. I didn't want to hear any more. From then on for the following year I was only half there.

My sister told me that Peter had been arrested for murder, but he was innocent. I thought immediately that he was a police victim. I would say to myself over and over again in the next few months: 'I wish I had kept my life simple and kept going to church.'

In July I had a week in Monklands Psychiatric Hospital, but when I was there I knew what I was doing. I was looking for an answer, some form of consolation there. I then realised that this was not where I was going to get it. Looking around at the people who were in there, I said to myself: 'I have got to get out of here and face life and I have to face what has happened to Peter.'

Believing Peter was innocent, it was terrible, a real nightmare. I thought that because of his left-wing politics and lifestyle, the police had probably had their eye on his group and that Peter had been a victim. Peter was in the pub when he was told about the boy's death and he appeared to be really shocked. Everybody remembered how shocked he looked.

Back in Glasgow something very important happened. Tim recognised at last that he had an alcohol problem. I think that what had happened to Peter sparked it off, bringing on Tim's guilt. He went to a self-help organisation and I also went to one, to deal with the problems that I had with Tim's drinking.

I heard Peter's story only in bits and pieces; we were up in Scotland and it was all happening in London. That was a mercy, too, because it avoided notoriety in Cumbernauld and Glasgow. Today I am grateful for that.

Peter got a very good lawyer who was sure that the police just wanted a conviction, and said he would fight for him. We were very pleased because from April until December, we were living every day believing he would have to face a trial at the Old Bailey. It was all totally foreign to me. I had never been within a yard of a court in my life. Of course my brothers had had mild run-ins with the police and the boys had had run-ins at football games. We had all developed this great animosity to the police, which is justified in some cases, but now we tarred them all with the same brush.

At first there was always something happening. People would be phoning and Douglas was coming up a lot. Then Peter was charged with murder and the words sounded so terrible. I still thought he had just been foolish and silly, because he said he did not do it and somebody else must have. There was a wee, wee bit of me, down in the corner of my heart which thought, he must have done it; I think he has. I don't know why it was there, but it was.

In December, Peter suddenly decided to open up and say that he was guilty. One morning he just made up his mind that he was going to tell the first person who visited him that day what he had done. He told the whole story to one of his friends. Douglas came up from London to tell me. Douglas always had a lot of bad feelings for his dad, but really he was just transferring my feelings on to himself. That relationship improved when Tim stopped drinking.

Even then I thought that Peter was still innocent and he was just saying that he had done it. In fact the truth was that the boy who had been killed had given Peter £200 to pay an electricity bill. Peter gambled it away, and got up the courage to tell him. The boy gave him another £200 and he gambled it away again. That was the ostensible reason for the killing. He could not face his friends. I can understand: it is the opposite of using a sprat to catch a mackerel; it is using a mackerel to catch a sprat. That is how I explain it in my mind. It was just immature and childlike. I still really do not like going over it. I just try to take life a day at a time. I could not take it in when it happened and I am only now gradually facing it.

Peter was a nervous boy. We were all affected by Tim's drinking and my reaction to it over the years. That gave me a terrible complex after Peter committed his crime because I thought it was really to do with family tensions and that it was me who should have been in prison and not Peter.

In the beginning I could not even say the word 'murder' about Peter's crime. I tried not to let words like 'knife' and 'murder' even come into my mind. There are no words to explain how you feel when a thing like that touches your life, when your son takes a human life. I try to think that is what happens in war, but this is different, this is personal.

Peter spent a year on remand in Brixton Prison. All his friends were supporting him; even when he confessed, they still maintained that support. Every day somebody went up to see him and brought him a meal so that he did not have to eat prison food.

I used to cry about it all, but I did not want to cry about it too much, because I felt that really it was my fault. Then I would think about the fire and think that what he went through then might have affected his brain. But I knew he had had a gambling problem before the fire. Then I would read about some new theory about schizophrenia in the good Sunday papers and wonder if that was the problem.

I think of Peter during those months in prison when he said he was innocent. He must have suffered terribly to keep up the pretence. With his friends coming in and reassuring him that he was a victim, it must have been awful. I was glad that he had the courage to come out and say: 'I did it.'

I feel that Peter has come a long way. He was very ill when he was in Brixton. He was crying and it was terrible to visit him. It really affected me all the time. When I was at home and made myself a cup of tea, I would think to myself that Peter could not just go and make himself a cup of tea, and I would immediately feel that I did not want to live. I despised myself because I didn't have the courage to end my life. People would say that I had my life to lead, which was separate from Peter's, but I would think they were talking nonsense. I felt terribly guilty, as if taking my own life would undo what Peter had done.

We went down to London regularly to visit Peter in prison, and his friends helped us with the fares. I always wanted to ask him how could he have done it, and I would find everything else difficult because that was what I wanted to know. I felt that I had to be brave enough to say it, but I would come away from the visit still not having said it. Then I learnt to let it go. It was up to him; he was under no obligation to justify himself to me. I was not his judge.

We kept in touch all the time by letter. At first I found that difficult. I could not write anything. I sat down to write, put down 'Dear Peter,' but I couldn't think of anything else to say. At that time Tim and I were having a lot of problems, but I remember him trying to make me write a letter to Peter, and I resented it. I wrote about half a dozen lines about nothing and then gradually it got easier.

His trial was more or less a formality. We went to it but it was like something in a nightmare. I was caught up in something that was so big I could not possibly understand it. I was not being assertive and, when I was, it was in the wrong way, like getting irritable. I was keeping up an appearance, because I saw myself as someone who had to be strong and brave, but it was not me.

Even then I was the perfectionist mother. I felt that when Peter came into the court he should have acted differently, he should not have held his head up so high. As if it mattered! But I felt that he should have been showing more remorse.

He was sent to Weyland Prison in Norfolk and he kept himself active. He is interested in people and he has a good command of the English language. He started an Open University course and enjoyed doing that. But what saved him was drama. He is the driving force behind the drama group in prison and he had a middle-page picture and article in the *Guardian*. He has done about half a dozen plays; he did one of Harold Pinter's and one about Scott of the Antarctic. I saw Joe Orton's *Loot*, which was brilliant. Beryl Bainbridge wrote it up and praised it in the *Oldie* magazine.

Peter is getting a second chance at life and I feel that I

got one, too. The self-help group which began to help me deal with my problems about Tim's drinking ended up looking at the difficulties I was having running my life and trying to run other people's.

For a while I used to think that I just could not take everything that had happened to me. Then I learnt, through the self-help group, to accept myself and appreciate my good qualities and to be honest about my wee faults and my big faults. I felt I needed all this because of the terrible thing that had happened to Peter, and I always put it in the passive. But Peter is a responsible human being and he is culpable. Being addicted to alcohol or gambling or being a member of a family where alcoholism is a problem is not an extenuating circumstance in a capital crime, but I think it ought to be. But that would mean an ideal state where everybody could be considered individually, and I realise the law has got to stop short of that simply to be efficient.

I am still coming to terms with what he did. It comes and it goes. The important thing is that I can come to terms with the fact that this was my son and he took another human life. All the tensions that affected Peter as a son and a brother and his relationship with his father and me all contributed to that. I cannot absolve him from what he did but with all this understanding I accept it.

The parents of one of Peter's friends in London heard about it. Although we had never met, they came and visited us, and that was one of the nicest things that happened. The husband said that it could have happened to his own son, because he felt we were all capable of doing something like that. That was a real boost.

At the beginning, every morning, I would wake up and have to face what Peter had done all over again. For the first eight months there was the compensating feeling that Peter was innocent. After he confessed, it was like a double shock.

Everybody has to take their share of the blame because no man is an island. It helped me to understand that the event had come from the problems within the family, but it did not help to take too much blame. Now I try not to dwell too much on the past. I just remember the nice things and the good times. I cope with life one day at a time.

I try not to make plans for when Peter comes out. Obviously I think about it, but I try to put it to the back of my mind. At the moment, my life is revolving around my youngest son, Michael, whose partner is having a baby soon. It will be my first grandchild.

Peter's crime has brought the family together because each one of us had to look at ourselves and our relationships with each other. At first it drew us all apart, because no one could accept the horror of it. We were all at sixes and sevens with each other. When something as dramatic as that happens, it knocks you back. You have to gradually come to terms with it. Some people want to go in right away. A bit of me is like that at times and Douglas is a 'let it all hang out' kind of person. He is all for getting in touch with your emotions, but he overrides other people because he thinks everyone should do it. He can be a bit extreme and come on too strong and this caused a bit of bother. Of course he was very loyal, visiting Peter often, but he got fanatical about Peter being in prison. He thinks prison is not the place to come to terms with yourself and he used to depress Tim and me because he saw it all from one side.

It is only in the last couple of years that the family has come together. Douglas was living down south anyway but Michael was still with us. He has seen Peter only once. He deals indirectly with him. He is interested, but I think there is a wee bit of withdrawing there. Michael does not want to be told too much about it. The old me would have tried to sort that out, but I can't, and I realise that now. He still considers himself part of the family and wants to hear news about Peter.

I am longing for Peter to come out, but I realise he will not be coming to live at home in Cumbernauld. He has a wee while to go yet. Before he comes out, he will have home visits and I am looking forward to the firt one. He has decided that he is going to come here for his first home visit. There was a little problem about that because he is in a prison down south, and because he was living in London when he was arrested, that is considered to be his official home. Now, I know he is not a wee baby who needs his mammy, he is a 33-year-old man, but I still feel it right that he comes home to his family for his first visit.

So far he has been out twice with a prison officer. The first time he went to Norwich Arts Centre to give a lecture on drama in prison and then he went to Norwich Library to establish a link between the library and the drama group.

He is a model prisoner, they say, which I think is fine and I hope it means he will be out sooner. Douglas thinks that Peter has not faced up to the enormity of what he did, but how can he know that? Douglas has got to learn to get on with his life and deal with his problems and to let Peter go.

What happened with Peter made me grow up. It was as if it were something I needed. It has made me more interested in people and less self-obsessed and small-minded. I do not practise any religion and I do not go to any church or chapel, but I think perhaps there is a higher power up there which makes something of life for us to follow through. We do have willpower and there are certain ways we can act. When it happened in 1984 I was at the height of the menopause, and it was all mixed up with that. For a while my thinking was distorted. When I was recovering from that stay in a mental hospital I thought back to how I had imagined, as a teenager, my life was going to be when I first got married: a beautiful husband, beautiful children and everything I had ever wanted. I compared that to what life had really been like. I was glad that I was able to say that there is a sense in which I have no regrets. Of course, like everyone, I have some, but they do not obsess me any more. I think that meant an easing of my guilt. It made me more honest, because there was less pretence in my life. Of course I wish Peter had never done it, but the effects of his crime on the family have not all been bad.

Theresa

'Theresa' lives with her husband, Angus, in a Suffolk seaside town. She has chosen to remain anonymous and all names have been changed. Her son, James, is serving life for the murder of the landlord of the pub next door to their seaside flat. She has another son, Gordon, who is in the merchant navy. Gordon is married and has given his parents two grandchildren, but to their sorrow they have lost touch with James's daughter, who is now a teenager. When Theresa met me at the station she seemed happy and relaxed. She was smartly dressed in her Sunday best, having just come from the local church, where Songs of Praise had been recorded, and as we walked through the town to her flat on the sea front we were greeted by many of the people in the town. Theresa resembles a bird – bright and chirpy with a slight figure and thin arms and legs; rather restless, constantly moving. Underneath that brightness is a mother devastated by both the actions of her son and the punishment he is having to bear. She told me that she keeps up her cheerful front because people who are depressed and feel sorry for themselves are not attractive and she does not want to be a drain on other people. She still manages to do voluntary work in a hospice in the local town. Her husband has been disabled by a series of strokes and has difficulty walking, so he is mostly confined to his chair in the sitting room, where he watches sport on television and has a telescope to look over the cliffs and out to sea. The emotional stress has taken a terrible physical toll on Theresa. She is frail and is undergoing a series of brain scans in hospital because the doctors believe *that she has suffered from minor strokes. Every day is spent worrying about James.*

When James was born, we were living in Rugby. My husband, Angus, was an electrical engineer and we already had one son, Gordon, who was three. The birth was terrible and I had to have a Caesarian. I did not see James for eight days after he was born as the doctors were worried about me and could not get my blood pressure down.

James was a lovely baby. He was walking at nine months and he was a real little daredevil. You name it and it would happen to him. One day Gordon was with a friend and they were playing with a dog. James bent down to stroke it and, of course, it bit him, which meant he had to have an injection in his bottom. Later, on a Sunday morning we were lying in bed at about seven in the morning when Gordon came in and said: 'James's outside on the patio.' He was three years old and had jumped twelve feet from the bedroom window. He was sitting on the patio without a bruise on him.

We used to come down here, to Suffolk, to visit my parents at half-terms and during the holidays. At the bottom of our garden there was a wood and one day Gordon came screaming up the garden shouting: 'You'll have to come, Daddy. James is caught up a tree.' James was hanging in the air by his corduroy trousers. When we took him to the hospital he had to have seven stitches in his scrotum. If he had not been wearing thick trousers I dread to think what he would have done to himself. The doctor asked him if he had had anything to eat and he said, 'Yes, a lollipop.' So the doctor said he could not have an anaesthetic. I had to hold on to his feet while the nurse held on to his head and the doctor tried to stitch him. He broke two needles and James was screaming his head off. Finally the doctor agreed to give him some anaesthetic.

The boys went to a prep school up the lane which had a smart uniform. It was a mauve blazer with yellow braid and a mauve cap with yellow piping round the edge. One day I was coming down the lane from shopping in town and I saw James with his play clothes on. I wondered how he had managed to get into the house to change. When I got home I discovered that he had broken a pane in the French windows, put his hand through and turned the key to get in. That was bad enough, but the reason he had come home to change was because he had a large L-shaped rip in his new blazer. He had tried to hide it so I wouldn't see it.

Then he had a serious accident. My mother and father had been staying and we were about to drive them back to Suffolk one Sunday. James decided that he wanted an Airfix kit, and rode his bicycle to the shop. After buying the plane, he was just cycling home when he was hit by a car. His head went through the windscreen and he had a compound fracture of his femur. If the doctor had not been living nearby James would not be here today. We were lucky: a woman who saw the accident recognised James because her son went to the same school and rang us. By the time we got there, the ambulance had taken him to hospital. He was in such a terrible state that they would not operate on him for twelve hours. After the operation, he was in a coma and on the critical list for four days. He was in hospital for about nineteen weeks. He even ended up with his picture in the hospital brochure.

He always picked a hobby that included dirt. When he was a young man he went pot-holing and when he came home everything was stiff. He wore his wetsuit underneath his clothes and he was filthy. I used to hear about all those accidents in pot-holes and I used to think, why can't he have another hobby? Then he started go-kart racing and he would always come off and hurt himself. When he played rugby, we would always be fetching him from the hospital with a cut hand or a cut head.

James did not like school. All he wanted to do was farm and he went to agricultural school. For experience, he worked at a marvellous large farm where he was very happy, but then it was taken over by somebody else who brought in his own people and didn't want James. He moved to a smaller farm, but it did not quite work out. James was always telling them a better way of doing things and they did not have the money they had at the other farm. By this time, we have moved to Cheshire, where Angus was running an electrical shop. He took James on.

James got married when he was only 21. Neither of them was ready for it. His wife, Jane, had stayed on at school and played netball for Cheshire. She seemed to think that money grew on trees, just like him. They didn't have any money and lived with us. Their daughter, Josie, was born and Jane worked right up until Josie was due. James wanted a much larger salary, but his father could not afford it. He could only pay him as an unmarried man. However they bought a house and moved into it when Josie was about eight months old. We still seemed to have Josie more than they did as they were always out. Then they moved down to Hampshire and that was when things started to go wrong between them. We went down to visit them occasionally and had Josie to stay.

My husband, Angus, had a stroke. I did not tell either of the boys what had happened for two weeks, because I was not sure how serious it was. The doctors gave me very little information. I decided to say that he had high blood pressure but James phoned the shop asking for his father, and the manager told him he was in hospital with a heart attack. That was the last thing I wanted him to know, because I knew what would happen: he would come rushing up and have an accident on Spaghetti Junction. I know what he is like driving a car. Gordon had joined the merchant navy by this time and was at sea. He rang when he docked in London for shore leave and came up but I told him not to stay because he would worry his father more if he did not rejoin his ship.

James decided to come up and stay for a while. Angus sort of improved but then he had another stroke. James went back down to Hampshire. We could not go down there because Angus could not travel. We realised that Angus was never going to fully recover. By that time we had a house here in Suffolk as well as Cheshire and we had the electrical shop. We could not afford the business and the other house, and we had to do something because we had no money coming in. We decided that we would come back here, to Suffolk, because we had always wanted to retire here, but Angus found our house here too difficult because of all the stairs. We found this flat, which has a lift and still looks over the sea.

James was already separated from Jane and he decided that he needed to be near his father, because he thought looking after Angus was too much for me. He packed up, came up here with no job to go to, and decorated the flat for us.

It was 1983 and a very hot summer. On the corner, just next door to this flat, is a pub. We knew he used to drink there a lot but we had no idea he was having an affair with Tracey, the landlady. He started working behind the bar, which we knew about, but we did not have an inkling about anything else. Everybody else seemed to know about it because they all told us afterwards, but it is too late afterwards. She was a married woman with two children. Everybody knew what Tracey was: she did not want a conversation with a woman, she was only interested in men. She would wear these tight jeans and boots with her hair up and she would just strut about like that.

One morning, I think it was a Thursday, I looked out of the window and there were police everywhere. The end of the road was blocked off. James had not been home. I went out by the back entrance of the flat because the police had closed off the front. I went into the newsagent's to get the paper, but when I asked what was going on the newsagent said he didn't know. So I went into the greengrocer's, which is nearby, and said: 'There's something funny going on.'

The girl said: 'Didn't you know? Barry, the landlord at the Coach and Horses, has been killed.' All of a sudden I felt myself go cold. She continued: 'And then there is that lad that works there.'

'I beg your pardon,' I said. 'That isn't some lad, that's my son.' My knees went. I said: 'Why, what's the matter?'

'He's in hospital.'

That was the first I knew. On the way back home I stopped to talk to the police. I told them who I was and then I asked what was going on. They got hold of my arms because I must have looked as though I was going to pass out, and they brought me home. The young policeman who brought me explained what had happened and said: 'I'll go and make arrangements to take you to the hospital.'

When we got there, James was semi-conscious and there was a detective by the bed waiting for him to come round to ask him questions. I asked the police to leave him alone because he was not in any fit state for questioning.

I thought that the person who'd murdered Barry had injured James, but I found out later that this was the way it was supposed to look. In fact Tracey had pushed James down the basement stairs and thrown a tray of glasses over him after they had killed her husband. She had planned to make it look like an intruder had got in and burgled the pub. There were bruises all over his body and we thought it was a wonder he was alive.

When I picked him up from hospital, we had to go to the police station to give a statement and we were kept there all afternoon. That evening two detectives came round and asked James all sorts of questions. He had to draw them plans of the inside and outside of the pub and explain what had happened by using the plans.

He went back to doing up the flat as usual, and working in the bar, as if nothing had happened. They searched our house, because an awful lot of money had been stolen, but we still did not know that it was James. We didn't even know he had been carrying on with Tracey, because we just did not go round in those circles.

It was Tracey they were after. The head of the CID said that they knew she was overreacting and that she had made up a story about seeing three youths running across the road in the dark. He knew she was lying and that Tracey and James had done it. The police had been hunting here, there and everywhere for evidence. They had searched the area where the youths were supposed to have been seen but could not find any trace of footprints in the grass or any signs of them climbing through the scrub on the headland in front of the pub.

One Saturday, about a month later, I came back from the hairdresser's to be told that the police had taken James to the police station. It got to nine o'clock and I still had no idea what was happening. I rang the police station. I kept saying, 'My son's had nothing to eat. I want to know when he is coming home.'

The police said they were coming over to see me, but I said that I didn't want to see them, I just wanted to know what time they were bringing my son home. They just went on telling me that someone would come and see me, but no one did.

It was on the local radio the next morning: the bulletin said that they had arrested several people in connection with the murder. Yet still I never thought it was my son. At last two policemen came round and one said: 'I suppose you know what we have come for?'

I said: 'I have no idea.'

He told me that they were holding James on suspicion of being involved in Barry's murder. I said that I thought they had badgered him and forced a confession out of him because they had been questioning him for so long and needed to arrest somebody.

The policeman said, far from it. He felt it was a relief for James to finally be able to tell somebody. We were all terribly upset. I cried and was in quite a state for a while. The policeman asked if I would like to go and see him and of course I said yes. He had told the policeman he would quite understand if I did not want to see him, which upset me. I felt so sick. We just could not believe it. I thought, oh God, I've got to get out.

The first person I saw was an acquaintance. I started to walk past her and she stopped me, saying: 'Aren't you going to speak to me?'

'I thought you would rather not speak to me.'

'Nonsense. I have know you since you were so high,' she replied. She was right. And she had known James since he was a baby. That was the way everybody treated me, and I have had no hostility whatsoever. The gossip was about what a slut Tracey was and everybody felt James had been duped.

When I went to see him, he just broke down because he had been charged. I thought that he could not possibly have done it and asked him about the youths Tracey had seen running away. He told me that she had made it all up. In fact he was prepared to lie for her and take all the blame because he was so besotted by her. If his solicitor and the two policemen had not interfered, he would have taken the rap for the lot, because he thought so much of her. She had not confessed because she was trying to push the blame on to James.

He never told me very much about it, except that she had already asked another man to do it, but he had refused. It was all to get her husband's life insurance. James told me that they had discussed the plan and he had said: 'You can't do that, it's murder!' She just said: 'Well, we won't get found out.'

James did hit him, but then he stopped, and she suffocated him. She told James that he had to finish him off but she hit him with a candlestick. The police could not find the weapon for ages – she had put it in the bath and scrubbed it and hid it inside the duvet in her little girl's bed. Then she tried to burn it on an electric stove in an empty flat, and what she could not burn, she threw over the cliffs.

Years later, when I was visiting James in prison, he told me that he did not like Barry, but that might have been based on what Tracey had told him, because he did not know him very well. She said he had made her pose for pornographic photos for magazines.

I went every day to his trial at the Crown Court. I was down in the court room, beneath the public gallery, which meant I did not have to see any of the public, which I appreciated. James was three seats away from me, and I could see him all the time. After the court adjourned each day, I could spend some time with him before I went for my train. I always thought he would get done for manslaughter and he pleaded not guilty to both murder and manslaughter. During the trial I took him clean shirts and sandwiches. I thought the trial was going very well, but when the judge was summing up, you would not have thought it was the same case. He was much more on her side. I wanted to get up and say: 'What's going on?' but the barrister kept pulling me down.

When James was in the witness box, they were asking him questions and I was hoping and praying he would give the right answers, which he did. But when the judge summed up, it was totally different from the case we had sat and listened to all week. I told James's barrister that I felt like writing to the head of the judges to complain. The judge was insulting to the barrister, and he got a letter of apology because the judge was sarcastic about some point he was trying to get over. The barrister was very good.

I passed out when the judge gave him a life sentence and I did not hear the rest. I had been feeling ill all day, because I had been dreading him being sentenced. I remember coming round in the hallway, and the junior barrister had a cup of tea for me. I had hoped, in my heart of hearts, that James would get off. The detective telephoned me the next morning to say that he was going on holiday, but if there was anything he could do for me, at any time, I must not hesitate to get in touch. He asked me if I was surprised at the sentence. I said that I was, because I had not thought James would get a life sentence – I thought the police were with him, not against him. I thought they were after her.

She got life, too, and four years extra, to run concurrently, for hiding the weapon – they called it withholding evidence. During the trial the jury had been sent out and her barrister had asked that she be tried only for withholding evidence because her barrister was saying that James had done it all. I was just furious.

After her husband's murder, before I knew the truth, I had even felt sorry for her and looked after her two young girls. When I took them out, the younger one said: 'My daddy's not coming back.'

Apparently, when Tracey phoned her mother-in-law and told her what had happened to Barry, the mother-in-law said it must have been her who had done it. After the trial the police said that if she had been an actress, she would have got an Oscar. I went every day to the trial and by God, they were right. She had an expression on her face as if she could not have done anything wrong but I knew otherwise.

I think people thought that she would not have been able to kill Barry, because she was not strong enough, being a woman, but she was a keep fit fanatic. If I had got hold of Tracey I would have hung, drawn and quartered her. When I heard she was going to appeal, I decided that if she got out I would kill her. The police were up in arms because after she was found guilty she appealed, but they were convinced that she would not succeed because of James's evidence against her. She lost it – and another subsequent appeal.

My friends have been marvellous. When James was on remand, it was a really difficult journey because of the trains. Some friends used to take me every fortnight, which was how often I was allowed to visit, while he was on remand.

Later he was transferred to the most deplorable place. On my first visit there I was physically sick. He was badly treated. Some of the officers had taken him to a cell on his own and beaten him up. Then he was transferred to the hospital wing. When I used to visit him there it was terrible. I had only fifteen minutes once a fortnight. I used to travel all the way, just for fifteen minutes – hardly enough time to get through the hellos. The visiting room was awful, with a disgusting floor. Even a pigsty would be better than that place. I could not even hug him because there was a long table, and we had to sit on either side of it, and there was a piece of glass along the middle of it. He was not in a very good state: he was not eating, and had lots of infections. I was very worried about him. When I suggested that he went to church on Christmas Day, he said that the prison guards could not be bothered to fetch people for it. I told our chaplain here, who had been to college with the prison chaplain, and he made sure James was able to go to church at Christmas, so that he could do something uplifting, even if it was just singing carols.

I found my first visit to James after the trial very tough. I was so upset I had to have a brandy. He had been sent to a different prison and when I got there, I looked up at it and thought that at least it could not be as bad as the last one. It looked modern, but that was just the front and really it is an old prison. I looked at the place where James was going to spend years and I was going to have to come month after month and my heart sank. I must have looked dazed and about to collapse because the prison officer said to me, 'Don't go into the visiting room like that because it will rub off on him. Don't go and hide away in a corner.' He showed me what to do and where to get tickets for the tea and coffee. Afterwards I thanked him for being on duty that day. Otherwise I do not know how I would have coped.

I had travelled by train and I had miles and miles of journey with nobody to talk to, either on the way up or when I came out. I used to sit on that train and think, whatever did he do that for? How did he get involved? I would wonder if I had gone wrong somewhere. It just went over and over in my mind.

At the prison he got a job in the education department and he was there when Princess Anne visited, but he was not allowed to see her. He started working in the officers' canteen, where he used to make all their bacon sandwiches, and the attitude of the officers there at that time was different. Two of them used to keep an eye out for him and I still write to one of them, because without those two I don't know what would have happened to James.

While most people around here have been marvellous we have had some funny phone calls. We were sat here one Sunday evening when the phone went and it was Acklington Prison. A man said he was phoning to tell me that my son had been moved to Acklington and I would be hearing from him later. I told my husband that I knew he wanted to move but I was surprised it was all the way there. Where he was was bad enough to get to, never mind Northumberland. The man said the decision was an internal one. We always send a letter on the Monday and his father puts in a few lines. I thought that we had better send him some money as he would have nothing when he got there, and I posted a £10 postal order.

The next day I got a letter from James postmarked as usual and I thought he must have written it before he moved. But in the letter he said he was just about to watch *Rugby Special*, which did not start until five. I thought it was a bit odd and I started feeling queer and cold when I realised someone had been messing about with us. Even though it was first thing in the morning, I had a brandy.

I telephoned the prison and asked if James was still there. The clerk who answered the telephone said: 'He was ten minutes ago. He has just brought me a mug of tea.' I told him what had happened and he said it was a hoax. Unfortunately, he told James how upset I was and by eleven that morning I had had both James and the welfare officer on the telephone. James was very upset to think they had got at me. When I next went to visit I was told that they knew it was one of the prison officers who had done it. I was terribly worried this man would start beating James up. I made an appointment with the governor, who said he would deal with it, but that man was not moved the whole time James was there. So the worry was always at the back of our minds until James left.

When James was due for his move, he was not given it straight away. I telephoned the Home Office to ask about it. I was told that he was near the top of the list, but I said it was not near enough the top for me. They told me to put it in writing and I told them what the prison was like. It was really horrible. You could cut the atmosphere with a knife, although it is a brand-new prison. It is pleasant inside, because they have got their own washbasins and toilets but the atmosphere worries me. I felt the prisoners were just waiting for a balloon to burst and something terrible to happen, and the officers were aggravating it. They did things like withholding prisoners' mail; James was always going on about his mail. There is nothing more distressing for somebody in a place like that than not receiving mail when they know letters are being sent. We used to have to be careful to date all the letters. About three weeks after I telephoned the Home Office, James was moved to where he is now.

That has its own problems. When he moved down there I was worried that he was going to just snap. They had James counselling attempted suicides, and I was worried he might do it himself. I just feel powerless because I cannot do anything.

Recently, James saw Tracey's photograph in one of the prison magazines because she had raised money for something. One of the officers had tried to cover it up, but it was too late, he had seen it. The welfare people asked him if he would like to write to her and possibly meet her. They do not understand that she lied to him.

I never even thought of not supporting him. He is my son and he always will be, and I always want to do the best for him. When I go and see him, it is lovely. He is just like he was before. He is full of remorse because he knows what he has done. Where he is now, he is a hospital orderly and a trustee. It was the same before, and when he left, some of the prison officers came up to me and said that they didn't want to lose him.

Gordon was stunned, because we had just told him it was a punch-up and that James was being done for grievous bodily harm. We wrote to him, but we did not tell him very much. When he came home he said: 'Well, what's he done, Mum? Is it GBH?' He has not been to see James

211

since he has been moved, because it is too far. Gordon has only had one leave for six weeks. He has his own life and house that he also has to deal with. He used to go with me when he was on leave before. He thinks James has been very stupid and if he had just stopped to think he would not have done it. He says he let his heart overrule his head.

If James had stopped and thought it out, I am sure he would never have done it. She must have had him round her little finger. That is also the only way I can think of it. It was just so out of character, as he was not an aggressive person.

I don't know if his daughter even knows about it because we lost contact with James's ex-wife and my granddaughter. Jane's boyfriend said he did not think Josie should see her father any more because it upset her and they would not give us their new address.

I still cannot believe what James has done. That woman was so devious. Everybody who knew her was aware of what she was like, but we didn't know because we had nothing to do with her. I occasionally see James's barrister, because of a lifeboat charity I work for, and he always makes a point of talking to me. He just says that we all know what sort of a woman she was. When we first moved into this flat Tracey sent flowers to us, but we just thought she was being friendly. People say that James is welcome to return here to live, but if she came back she would be lynched.

I had to go and have a brain scan a month ago because I have been having black-outs. They were worried that I might have developed a tumour, but apparently I have had a series of minor strokes and I think the first time was when I blacked out after his trial. So James's crime has certainly taken its toll in more ways than one. And it has also had an effect on his father.

I feel it has ruined his life and it has ruined ours as well. We are also serving a sentence. It is always there at the back of your mind at any part of the day. Some people ask why we did not move away but we moved here that May for Angus to retire and it happened in the first week in

July. It never entered my head to move – I don't think Angus could stand the upheaval of moving again.

It is a nightmare really, a nightmare you just cannot get out of. James is 37 and has been in jail for nine years. We are hoping he will only serve another two years. First, he has got to move to Leyhill, which is an open prison near Bristol. However, we know someone who was sentenced to eight years and he has already done twelve so far, so we really do not know when to expect James back.

I think the justice and prison systems are awful. We did not think about it before, because it didn't affect us. However, now that I am involved I know it is rotten. There is no justice to protect the innocent. I still think he got the wrong sentence, but we cannot do anything about it. They never brought out what sort of a character she was.

There is no point in us being upset all the time because it would not be good for us. I am on committees and I go to church, but I did not start going to church just because of what James did. I just think to myself that they are not going to get me down. I could get bitter if I let myself. My sister does not ask after him, which hurts really, because if the boot had been on the other foot I would have been totally different. We are looking forward to James coming out. I never thought of disowning him, he is ours and that is it. I can remember feeling glad that my father was not alive because that would have finished him. He thought the world of James. My mother died some years previously. She came in from shopping and said: 'I've just bought something for James.' Then she went out and had a massive heart attack.

The last time I went to see James he told me he was working through his remorse by helping other people, because he is counselling for the Samaritans. Prisoners will talk to James while they would not talk to an officer. He is on the hospital wing, working with civilians, that is, nurses who are employed by the prison but are not part of the prison, so he is mixing with good people. He said: 'I don't cause any problems, I just want to get to do my time and get out of here.'

I am trying to encourage him to go in for counselling when he comes out. Prisons employ a lot of counsellors – it is the up-and-coming thing that they want to do.

As the years go on I keep wondering if I am going to be here when he comes out. I don't know if he will settle here – I think he might settle down south because he has friends there who visit him, which is marvellous, really. We have twice discussed whether he will come back here and he asked me if I would be terribly upset if he didn't. I can see his point, really.

Appendix

Aftermath PO Box 414, Sheffield S1 3UP. Tel: 0742 326166.

Andrew Lee Jones Fund (Assisting Lawyers for Justice on Death Row) 1 Hemyock Road, Selly Oak, Birmingham B29 4DG. Tel: 021-475 4344.

Howard League for Penal Reform Tel: 071-281 7722.

Justice Tel: 071-405 6018.

National Association for the Care and Rehabilitation of Offenders (NACRO) Tel: 071-582 6500.

New Bridge Tel: 081-976 0779.

Prison Reform Trust Tel: 071-278 9815.

Trauma After Care Trust Tel: 0242 890306.

Victim Support Tel: 071-735 9166.

References

Home Office 1991a *Prison Disturbances*, April 1990 (Woolf Report), HMSO.

Light, R. (ed) *Prisoners' Families* (1989), Bristol and Bath Centre for Criminal Justice.

Light, R. (ed) *Prisoners' Families: Keeping in Touch* (1992), Bristol Centre for Criminal Justice.

Matthews, J. *Forgotten Victims* (1983), NACRO.

McDermott, K. and King, R. D. *Prison Rule 102: 'Stand by Your Man' – The impact of penal policy on the families of prisoners.*

Morgan, R. *Woolf and Prisoners and their Families* (1992), conference paper from Light, R. (ed.), 1992.

DYING TO GET MARRIED
The Courtship and Murder of
Julie Miller Bulloch

by Ellen Harris

At 30, Julie Miller was a successful executive who dreamed of a white knight who would come and bring romance to her well-ordered life. Then, after placing an ad in a St Louis personal column, Julie met Dennis Bulloch. Movie-star handsome, an MBA, a member of the young Republicans, he seemed to be the perfect husband.

But underneath the perfect façade was a violent, disturbed man. A compulsive womaniser and social climber, Bulloch married Julie for her money and connections. Just ten weeks after their wedding, Julie's burnt body was discovered after a fire in the garage. Naked, she had been bound to a rocking chair with more than 76 feet of tape.

The shocking true story of Julie Miller Bulloch's desperate search for love and her tragic death is the story of an American dream that turned into a brutal nightmare.

ISBN 0 86369 638 4

THE BUTCHERS

by Brian Lane

Which is the most effective way to dispose of a corpse? Eat it? Dip it in acid? Feed it to pigs? Turn it into sausages? Or put it in the furnace?

These are among the tried and tested methods of the thirty cold-blooded killers in *The Butchers*, from Dennis Nilsen to Marcel Petiot and Albert Fish, who compounded their original crimes of murder with deliberate and macabre mutilations.

However meticulous and ingenious, none of them got away, but only painstaking investigation and forensics led to the final unmasking of the sadists and psychotics who sought such bloody concealment of their crimes.

ISBN 0 86369 600 7

DAMSEL OF DEATH

by Sue Russell

On Death Row in Florida is the rarest of criminals – a female serial killer.

Arrested in January 1991, Aileen Wuornos confessed to murdering seven men. Abandoned by her mother and abused by her grandfather, at eleven she had prostituted herself; at fourteen she became pregnant; and by thirty-three she had begun to kill. In this gripping true story, British journalist Sue Russell slices through the horror of America's underbelly to find out what made the quiet little girl from Michigan grow up into a multiple killer.

ISBN 0 86369 608 2

PRECIOUS VICTIMS

by Don W. Weber and Charles Bosworth Jr

Who would believe a mother could murder her own baby? It seemed the least likely explanation to the Jersey County police when they heard Paula Sims' story of a masked kidnapper in June 1986. But then, in April 1989, her second newborn daughter suffered an identical fate. This time the police would not stop searching until they had discovered the whole, horrifying truth.

Written by the lawyer who won the case, and the reporter who covered it from beginning to end, *Precious Victims* is a riveting journey into the twisted heart of a family with a dark and murderous secret.

ISBN 0 86369 598 1

THE SERIAL KILLERS

by Colin Wilson and Donald Seaman

White. Twenty-eight years old. High IQ. And a law student. Yuppie success story?

No, portrait of a serial killer. Ted Bundy, one of the most notorious serial killers of recent years, confessed to killing 23 women. But he was no aberration. Statistics show that most serial killers are young, white, intelligent males. Triggered by either sexual fantasies or a need to inflict pain and fear, their sadistic addiction to frenzied killing is the most horrifying of all crimes. And serial killers are increasing at an alarming rate.

But with the formation of the world's first National Centre for the Analysis of Violent Crime in Virginia, made famous in the hugely popular *The Silence of the Lambs*, the methods of tracking down these killers have been revolutionised.

Using their privileged access to the centre's sophisticated techniques of pyschological profiling, Colin Wilson and Donald Seaman have produced the most comprehensive study to date of this terrifying modern phenomenon. *The Serial Killers* is the definitive study of the psychology of the criminal mind.

ISBN 0 86369 615 5

LADYKILLER

by Christopher Berry-Dee
and Robin Odell

In July 1986, three days after John Guise Cannan was released following an eight-year sentence for rape, estate agent Suzy Lamplugh went alone to meet a prospective client. She was never seen again. In April 1989, after Cannan's conviction for the murder and rape of newlywed Shirley Banks, the judge recommended that he 'never again be at liberty outside of prison walls' and the Lamplugh file was finally closed. . .

Handsome and charming, John Cannan wooed women with flowers, champagne and flattery, and boasted of over a hundred one-night stands in three years. But how did such a violent man win his way into so many women's hearts? And what turned him into a vicious rapist who killed at least once?

Drawing on the latest psychological profiling knowledge developed in America by the FBI, and on an intense three-year correspondence between Cannan and the authors, *Ladykiller* provides a chillingly personal and comprehensive portrait of a complex and intelligent man. Rarely has a book delved so deeply into the mind of a convicted murderer.

'A balanced, sensitive psychological portrait'
Diana Lamplugh, *Mail on Sunday*

ISBN 0 86369 690 2

THE RED RIPPER

by Peter Conradi

He was a soft-spoken grandfather. The 'perfect' family man. A former Russian literature teacher. And a serial killer.

Beneath Andrei Chikatilo's model-citizen exterior lurked the warped mind of one of the most prolific killers of all time. At his 1992 trial, watched in his cage by the world's media, Chikatilo was convicted of murdering a horrifying total of 52 women and children over twelve years.

Peter Conradi, an English journalist based in Moscow, has interviewed key figures – from the police who finally caught Chikatilo (six years after an initial arrest in 1984) to the psychiatrist who helped track him down – to lay bare a damaged mind in a damaged society.

ISBN 0 86369 618 X